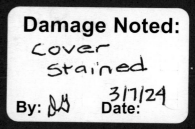

The Creative Act

A Way of Being

Rick Rubin

with Neil Strauss

PENGUIN PRESS · NEW YORK · 2023

PENGUIN PRESS
An imprint of Penguin Random House LLC
penguinrandomhouse.com

Library of Congress Cataloging-in-Publication Data

Names: Rubin, Rick, author. | Strauss, Neil, author.
Title: The creative act : a way of being / Rick Rubin, with Neil Strauss.
Description: New York : Penguin Press, 2023.
Identifiers: LCCN 2022035005 | ISBN 9780593652886 (hardcover) |
    ISBN 9780593653425 (ebook)
Subjects: LCSH: Creative ability. | Creation (Literary, artistic, etc.)
Classification: LCC BF408 .R7368 2023 | DDC 153.3/5—dc23/eng/20220921
LC record available at https://lccn.loc.gov/2022035005

Printed in the United States of America
5th Printing

Book design by Rick Rubin with special thanks to Pentagram

The object isn't to make art,
it's to be in that wonderful state
which makes art inevitable.

Robert Henri

78 Areas of Thought

Nothing in this book
is known to be true.
It's a reflection on what I've noticed—
Not facts so much as thoughts.

Some ideas may resonate,
others may not.
A few may awaken an inner knowing
you forgot you had.
Use what's helpful.
Let go of the rest.

Each of these moments
is an invitation
to further inquiry:
looking deeper,
zooming out, or in.
Opening possibilities
for a new way of being.

Everyone Is a Creator

(•)

Those who do not engage in the traditional arts might be wary of calling themselves *artists*. They might perceive creativity as something extraordinary or beyond their capabilities. A calling for the special few who are born with these gifts.

Fortunately, this is not the case.

Creativity is not a rare ability. It is not difficult to access. Creativity is a fundamental aspect of being human. It's our birthright. And it's for all of us.

Creativity doesn't exclusively relate to making art. We all engage in this act on a daily basis.

To create is to bring something into existence that wasn't

1

there before. It could be a conversation, the solution to a problem, a note to a friend, the rearrangement of furniture in a room, a new route home to avoid a traffic jam.

What you make doesn't have to be witnessed, recorded, sold, or encased in glass for it to be a work of art. Through the ordinary state of being, we're already creators in the most profound way, creating our experience of reality and composing the world we perceive.

In each moment, we are immersed in a field of undifferentiated matter from which our senses gather bits of information. The outside universe we perceive doesn't exist as such. Through a series of electrical and chemical reactions, we generate a reality internally. We create forests and oceans, warmth and cold. We read words, hear voices, and form interpretations. Then, in an instant, we produce a response. All of this in a world of our own creation.

Regardless of whether or not we're formally making art, we are all living as artists. We perceive, filter, and collect data, then curate an experience for ourselves and others based on this information set. Whether we do this consciously or unconsciously, by the mere fact of being alive, we are active participants in the ongoing process of creation.

To live as an artist is a way of being in the world. A way of perceiving. A practice of paying attention. Refining our sensitivity to tune in to the more subtle notes. Looking for what draws us in and what pushes us away. Noticing what feeling tones arise and where they lead.

Attuned choice by attuned choice, your entire life is a form of self-expression. You exist as a creative being in a creative universe. A singular work of art.

Tuning In

Think of the universe as an eternal creative unfolding.

Trees blossom.

Cells replicate.

Rivers forge new tributaries.

The world pulses with productive energy, and everything that exists on this planet is driven by that energy.

Every manifestation of this unfolding is doing its own work on behalf of the universe, each in its own way, true to its own creative impulse.

Just as trees grow flowers and fruits, humanity creates works of art. The Golden Gate Bridge, the *White Album,*

Guernica, Hagia Sophia, the Sphinx, the space shuttle, the Autobahn, "Clair de lune," the Colosseum in Rome, the Phillips screwdriver, the iPad, Philadelphia cheesesteak.

Look around you: there are so many remarkable accomplishments to appreciate. Each of these is humanity being true to itself, as a hummingbird is true to itself by building a nest, a peach tree by bearing fruit, and a nimbus cloud by producing rain.

Every nest, every peach, every raindrop, and every great work is different. Some trees may appear to make more beautiful fruits than others, and some humans may appear to compose greater works than others. The taste and beauty are in the eye of the beholder.

How does the cloud know when to rain? How does the tree know when spring begins? How does the bird know when it's time to build a new nest?

The universe functions like a clock:

To everything—

There is a season—

And a time to every purpose under heaven

A time to be born, a time to die

A time to plant, a time to reap

A time to kill, a time to heal

A time to laugh, a time to weep

A time to build up, a time to break down

A time to dance, a time to mourn

A time to cast away stones

A time to gather stones together

These rhythms are not set by us. We are all participating in a larger creative act we are not conducting. We are being conducted. The artist is on a cosmic timetable, just like all of nature.

If you have an idea you're excited about and you don't bring it to life, it's not uncommon for the idea to find its voice through another maker. This isn't because the other artist stole your idea, but because the idea's time has come.

In this great unfolding, ideas and thoughts, themes and songs and other works of art exist in the aether and ripen on schedule, ready to find expression in the physical world.

As artists, it is our job to draw down this information, transmute it, and share it. We are all translators for messages the universe is broadcasting. The best artists tend to be the ones with the most sensitive antennae to draw in the energy resonating at a particular moment. Many great artists first develop sensitive antennae not to create art but to protect themselves. They have to protect themselves because everything hurts more. They feel everything more deeply.

⊙

Often art arrives in movements. Bauhaus architecture, abstract expressionism, French New Wave cinema, Beat poetry, punk rock to name a few from recent history. These movements appear like a wave; some artists are able to read the culture and position themselves to ride that swell. Others might see the wave and choose to swim against the current.

We are all antennae for creative thought. Some transmissions come on strong, others are more faint. If your antenna isn't sensitively tuned, you're likely to lose the data in the noise. Particularly since the signals coming through are often more subtle than the content we collect through sensory awareness. They are energetic more than tactile, intuitively perceived more than consciously recorded.

Most of the time, we are gathering data from the world through the five senses. With the information that's being transmitted on higher frequencies, we are channeling energetic material that can't be physically grasped. It defies logic, in the same way that an electron can be in two places at once. This elusive energy is of great worth, though so few people are open enough to hold it.

How do we pick up on a signal that can neither be heard nor be defined? The answer is not to look for it. Nor do we attempt to predict or analyze our way into it. Instead, we create an open space that allows it. A space so free of the normal overpacked condition of our minds that it functions as a vacuum. Drawing down the ideas that the universe is making available.

This freedom is not as difficult to achieve as one might think. We all start with it. As children, we experience much less interference between receiving ideas and internalizing them. We accept new information with delight instead of making comparisons to what we already believe; we live in the moment rather than worrying about future consequences; we are spontaneous more than analytical; we are curious, not jaded. Even the most ordinary experiences in life are met with a sense of awe. Deep sadness and intense excitement can come within moments of each other. There's no facade and no attachment to a story.

Artists who are able to continually create great works throughout their lives often manage to preserve these childlike qualities. Practicing a way of being that allows you to see the world through uncorrupted, innocent eyes can free you to act in concert with the universe's timetable.

There's a time for certain ideas to arrive,
and they find a way
to express themselves through us.

*

*

*

*

*

*

*

The creative act : a way of being

31449005836756

Pickup By: 3/23/2024

BOUTIN, ERIKA
MARIE

The Source of Creativity

We begin with everything:

everything seen,

everything done,

everything thought,

everything felt,

everything imagined,

everything forgotten,

and everything that rests unspoken and unthought

within us.

This is our source material, and from it, we build each creative moment.

This content does not come from inside us. The Source is out there. A wisdom surrounding us, an inexhaustible offering that is always available.

We either sense it, remember it, or tune in to it. Not only through our experiences. It may also be dreams, intuitions, subliminal fragments, or other ways still unknown by which the outside finds its way inside.

To the mind, this material appears to come from within. But that's an illusion. There are tiny fragments of the vastness of Source stored within us. These precious wisps arise from the unconscious like vapor, and condense to form a thought. An idea.

⊙

It may be helpful to think of Source as a cloud.

Clouds never truly disappear. They change form. They turn into rain and become part of the ocean, and then evaporate and return to being clouds.

The same is true of art.

Art is a circulation of energetic ideas. What makes them appear new is that they're combining differently each time they come back. No two clouds are the same.

This is why, when we are struck by a new piece of art, it

can resonate on a deeper level. Perhaps this is the familiar, coming back to us in an unfamiliar form. Or maybe it *is* something unknown that we didn't realize we were looking for. A missing piece in a puzzle that has no end.

Turning something from an idea
into a reality
can make it seem smaller.
It changes from unearthly to earthly.

The imagination has no limits.
The physical world does.
The work exists in both.

Awareness

In most of our daily activities we choose the agenda and develop a strategy to achieve the goal at hand. We create the program.

Awareness moves differently. The program is happening around us. The world is the doer and we are the witness. We have little or no control over the content.

The gift of awareness allows us to notice what's going on around and inside ourselves in the present moment. And to do so without attachment or involvement. We may observe bodily sensations, passing thoughts and feelings, sounds or visual cues, smells and tastes.

Through detached noticing, awareness allows an observed flower to reveal more of itself without our intervention. This is true of all things.

Awareness is not a state you force. There is little effort involved, though persistence is key. It's something you actively allow to happen. It is a presence with, and acceptance of, what is happening in the eternal now.

As soon as you label an aspect of Source, you're no longer noticing, you're studying. This holds true of any thought that takes you out of presence with the object of your awareness, whether analysis or simply becoming aware that you're aware. Analysis is a secondary function. The awareness happens first as a pure connection with the object of your attention. If something strikes me as interesting or beautiful, first I live that experience. Only afterward might I attempt to understand it.

Though we can't change what it is that we are noticing, we can change our ability to notice.

We can expand our awareness and narrow it, experience it with our eyes open or closed. We can quiet our inside so we can perceive more on the outside, or quiet the outside so we can notice more of what's happening inside.

We can zoom in on something so closely it loses the features that make it what it appears to be, or zoom so far out it seems like something entirely new.

The universe is only as large as our perception of it. When we cultivate our awareness, we are expanding the universe.

This expands the scope, not just of the material at our disposal to create from, but of the life we get to live.

The ability to look deeply
is the root of creativity.
To see past the ordinary and mundane
and get to what might otherwise be invisible.

The Vessel and the Filter

⊙

Each of us has a container within. It is constantly being filled with data.

It holds the sum total of our thoughts, feelings, dreams, and experiences in the world. Let's call this the vessel.

Information does not enter the vessel directly, like rain filling into a barrel. It is filtered in a unique way for each of us.

Not everything makes it through this filter. And what does get through doesn't always do so faithfully.

We each have our own method of reducing Source. Our memory space is limited. Our senses often misperceive data. And our minds don't have the processing power to take in all the information surrounding us. Our senses would be over-whelmed by light, color, sound, and smell. We would not be able to distinguish one object from another.

To navigate our way through this immense world of data, we learn early in life to focus on information that appears essential or of particular interest. And to tune out the rest.

As artists, we seek to restore our childlike perception: a more innocent state of wonder and appreciation not tethered to utility or survival.

Our filter inevitably reduces Source intelligence by inter-preting the data that arrives instead of letting it pass freely. As the vessel fills with these recast fragments, relationships are created with the material already collected.

These relationships produce beliefs and stories. They may be about who we are, the people around us, and the nature of the world we live in. Eventually, these stories co-alesce into a worldview.

As artists, we want to hold these stories softly and find space for the vast amount of information that doesn't fit eas-ily within the limits of our belief system. The more raw data we can take in, and the less we shape it, the closer we get to nature.

⊙

One can think of the creative act as taking the sum of our vessel's contents as potential material, selecting for elements that seem useful or significant in the moment, and representing them.

This is Source drawn through us and made into books, movies, buildings, paintings, meals, businesses—whatever projects we embark on.

If we choose to share what we make, our work can recirculate and become source material for others.

Source makes available.
The filter distills.
The vessel receives.
And often this happens beyond our control.

It is helpful to know this default system can be bypassed. With training, we can improve our interface with Source and radically expand the vessel's ability to receive. Changing the instrument is not always the easiest way to change the sound of the music, but it can be the most powerful.

No matter what tools you use to create,
the true instrument is you.
And through you,
the universe that surrounds us
all comes into focus.

The Unseen

By conventional definition, the purpose of art is to create physical and digital artifacts. To fill shelves with pottery, books, and records.

Though artists generally aren't aware of it, that end work is a by-product of a greater desire. We aren't creating to produce or sell material products. The act of creation is an attempt to enter a mysterious realm. A longing to transcend. What we create allows us to share glimpses of an inner landscape, one that is beyond our understanding. Art is our portal to the unseen world.

Without the spiritual component, the artist works with a crucial disadvantage. The spiritual world provides a sense of wonder and a degree of open-mindedness not always found within the confines of science. The world of reason can be narrow and filled with dead ends, while a spiritual viewpoint is limitless and invites fantastic possibilities. The unseen world is boundless.

The word *spirituality* may not speak to those who dwell chiefly in the intellect or those who equate the word with organized religion. If you prefer to think of spirituality as simply believing in connection, that's fine. If you choose to think of it as believing in magic, that's fine too. The things we believe carry a charge regardless of whether they can be proven or not.

The practice of spirituality is a way of looking at a world where you're not alone. There are deeper meanings behind the surface. The energy around you can be harnessed to elevate your work. You are part of something much larger than can be explained—a world of immense possibilities.

Harnessing this energy can be marvelously useful in your creative pursuits. The principle operates on faith. Believing and behaving as if it's true. No proof is needed.

When you're working on a project, you may notice apparent coincidences appearing more often than randomness allows—almost as if there is another hand guiding yours in a certain direction. As if there is an inner knowing gently informing your movements. Faith allows you to trust the direction without needing to understand it.

Pay particular attention to the moments that take your

breath away—a beautiful sunset, an unusual eye color, a moving piece of music, the elegant design of a complex machine.

If a piece of work, a fragment of consciousness, or an element of nature is somehow allowing us to access something bigger, that is its spiritual component made manifest. It awards us a glimpse of the unseen.

It's not unusual for science
to catch up to art, eventually.
Nor is it unusual for art
to catch up to the spiritual.

Look for Clues

·

Material for our work surrounds us at every turn. It's woven into conversation, nature, chance encounters, and existing works of art.

When looking for a solution to a creative problem, pay close attention to what's happening around you. Look for clues pointing to new methods or ways to further develop current ideas.

A writer may be in a coffee shop, working on a scene and unsure what a character is going to say next. A phrase might be overheard in the chatter from another table that provides a direct answer, or at least a glimpse of a possible direction.

We receive these types of messages all the time, if we

remain open to them. We might read a book and find a quote leaping off the page, or watch a movie and notice a line that moves us to pause and rewind. Sometimes it's the exact answer we've been looking for. Or it could be an echo of an idea that keeps repeating in other places—begging for more attention or affirming the path we're on.

These transmissions are subtle: they are ever-present, but they're easy to miss. If we aren't looking for clues, they'll pass by without us ever knowing. Notice connections and consider where they lead.

When something out of the ordinary happens, ask yourself why. What's the message? What could be the greater meaning?

This process isn't a science. We can't control clues, or will them to be revealed. Sometimes it helps to have a strong intention to find a specific answer, or to confirm a particular path. Other times, letting go of that intention altogether can help you find your way.

An integral part of the artist's work is deciphering these signals. The more open you are, the more clues you will find and the less effort you'll need to exert. You may be able to think less and begin to rely on answers arising within you.

You might imagine that the outside world is a conveyor belt with a stream of small packages on it, always going by. The first step is to notice the conveyor belt is there. And then, any time you want, you can pick up one of those packages, unwrap it, and see what's inside.

A helpful exercise might be opening a book to a random page and reading the first line your eyes find. See how what's written there somehow applies to your situation. Any relevance it bears might be by chance, but you might allow for the possibility that chance is not all that's at play. When my appendix burst, the doctor who diagnosed it insisted that I go to the hospital immediately to have it removed. I was told there were no other options. I found myself in a nearby bookstore. Standing out on a table in the front was a new book by Dr. Andrew Weil. I picked it up and let it fall open. The first passage my eyes went to said: if a doctor wants to remove a part of your body, and they tell you it has no function, don't believe this. The information I needed was made available to me in that moment. And I still have my appendix.

When clues present themselves, it can sometimes feel like the delicate mechanism of a clock at work. As if the universe is nudging you with little reminders that it's on your side and wants to provide everything you need to complete your mission.

Look for what you notice
but no one else sees.

Practice

(•)

In the wild, animals must narrow their field of vision to survive. A tight focus prevents distraction from critical needs.

Food,

Shelter,

Predators,

Procreation.

For the artist, this reflexive action can be a hindrance. Widening one's scope allows for more moments of interest to be noticed and collected, building a treasury of material to draw from later.

A *practice* is the embodiment of an approach to a concept. This can support us in bringing about a desired state of mind. When we repeat the exercise of opening our senses to what is, we move closer to living in a continually open state. We build a habit. One where expanded awareness is our default way of being in the world.

To deepen this practice is to embark on a more profound relationship with Source. As we reduce the interference of our filter, we become better able to recognize the rhythms and movements around us. This allows us to participate with them in a more harmonious way.

When we take notice of the cycles of the planet, and choose to live in accordance with its seasons, something remarkable happens. We become connected.

We begin to see ourselves as part of a greater whole that is constantly regenerating itself. And we may then tap into this all-powerful propagating force and ride its creative wave.

⊙

To support our practice, we might set up a daily schedule, where we engage in particular rituals at specific times every day or week.

The gestures we perform don't need to be grand. Small rituals can make a big difference.

We can decide to take three slow, deep breaths upon awakening each morning. This simple act can set a course to start each day still, centered, and in the moment.

We might also eat our meals mindfully, slowly savoring

each bite with appreciation. Take a daily walk in nature, looking at everything entering our field of vision with gratitude and connection. Take a moment to marvel at the feeling of our heartbeat and the movement of blood through our veins before sleep.

The purpose of such exercises is not necessarily in the doing, just as the goal of meditation isn't in the meditating. The purpose is to evolve the way we see the world when we're not engaged in these acts. We are building the musculature of our psyche to more acutely tune in. This is so much of what the work is about.

Awareness needs constant refreshing. If it becomes a habit, even a good habit, it will need to be reinvented again and again.

Until one day, you notice that you are always in the practice of awareness, at all times, in all places, living your life in a state of constant openness to receiving.

Living life as an artist is a practice.
You are either engaging in the practice
or you're not.

It makes no sense to say you're not good at it.
It's like saying, "I'm not good at being a monk."
You are either living as a monk or you're not.

We tend to think of the artist's work as the
output.

The real work of the artist
is a way of being in the world.

Submerge
(The Great Works)

(•)

Broadening our practice of awareness is a choice we can make at any moment.

It is not a search, though it is stoked by a curiosity or hunger. A hunger to see beautiful things, hear beautiful sounds, feel deeper sensations. To learn, and to be fascinated and surprised on a continual basis.

In service of this robust instinct, consider submerging yourself in the canon of great works. Read the finest literature, watch the masterpieces of cinema, get up close to the most influential paintings, visit architectural landmarks. There's no standard list; no one has the same measures of greatness. The "canon" is continually changing, across time and space. Nonetheless, exposure to great art provides an invitation. It draws us forward, and opens doors of possibility.

If you make the choice of reading classic literature every day for a year, rather than reading the news, by the end of that time period you'll have a more honed sensitivity for recognizing greatness from the books than from the media.

This applies to every choice we make. Not just with art, but with the friends we choose, the conversations we have, even the thoughts we reflect on. All of these aspects affect our ability to distinguish good from very good, very good from great. They help us determine what's worthy of our time and attention.

Because there's an endless amount of data available to us and we have a limited bandwidth to conserve, we might consider carefully curating the quality of what we allow in.

This doesn't just apply if your goal is to make art of lasting significance. Even if your goal is to make fast food, it will likely taste better if you experience the best fresh food available to you during the process. Level up your taste.

The objective is not to learn to mimic greatness, but to calibrate our internal meter for greatness. So we can better make the thousands of choices that might ultimately lead to our own great work.

Nature as Teacher

(•)

Of all the great works that we can experience, nature is the most absolute and enduring. We can witness it change through the seasons. We can see it in the mountains, the oceans, the deserts, and the forest. We can watch the changes of the moon each night, and the relationship between the moon and the stars.

There is never a shortage of awe and inspiration to be found outdoors. If we dedicated our lives solely to noticing changes in natural light and shadow as the hours pass, we would constantly discover something new.

We don't have to understand nature to appreciate it. This

is true of all things. Simply be aware of moments when your breath gets taken away by something of great beauty.

It may be witnessing a single-line formation of birds snaking through a half-lit evening sky, or standing awed at the foot of a giant redwood tree that's thousands of years old. There's so much wisdom in nature that when we notice it, it awakens possibility within us. It is through communing with nature that we move closer to our own nature.

If you're picking colors based on a Pantone book, you're limited to a certain number of choices. If you step out in nature, the palette is infinite. Each rock has such a variation of color within it, we could never find a can of paint to mimic the exact same shade.

Nature transcends our tendencies to label and classify, to reduce and limit. The natural world is unfathomably more rich, interwoven, and complicated than we are taught, and so much more mysterious and beautiful.

Deepening our connection to nature will serve our spirit, and what serves our spirit invariably serves our artistic output.

The closer we can get to the natural world, the sooner we start to realize we are not separate. And that when we create, we are not just expressing our unique individuality, but our seamless connection to an infinite oneness.

There's a reason we are drawn
to gazing at the ocean.
It is said the ocean provides
a closer reflection of who
we are than any mirror.

Nothing Is Static

The world is always changing.

You can engage in the same awareness practice five days in a row in the same location and have a unique experience each time.

Different sounds and different smells may be present. No two gusts of wind feel quite the same. The tone and quality of sunlight changes from minute to minute and day to day.

Within the richness of nature, the variations are easily noticeable. Some are shouts, others whispers. Even if an element seems static, whether a work of art in a museum or an everyday object in a kitchen, when we look at it deeply, we can see a newness. We recognize aspects unnoticed before.

Reread the same book over and over, and we'll likely find new themes, undercurrents, details, and connections.

You can't step into the same stream twice because it's always flowing. Everything is.

The world is constantly changing, so no matter how often we practice paying attention, there will always be something new to notice. It's up to us to find it.

Likewise, we are always changing, growing, evolving. We learn and forget things. We move through different moods, thoughts, and unconscious processes. The cells in our body die and regenerate. No one is the same person all day long.

Even if the world outside were to remain static, the information we took in would still be ever-changing. And so too would the work we bring forth.

The person who makes something today
isn't the same person
who returns to the work tomorrow.

Look Inward

The sound of water churning in the distance is audible.

I feel a breeze of what might be warm air, though it's difficult to tell, since my arm hair senses the movement as cooling.

Two birds are singing and, with my eyes closed, I'm placing them approximately fifty paces behind me and to my right.

Now a smaller bird, or at least one with a smaller and higher pitched chirp, enters the soundscape behind me to the left. From the rhythmic interplay, it seems clear the birds are not in conversation. Each sings its own song.

I notice the sound of a passing vehicle and, in the distance, children's voices. A blur of rhythmic music arrives from the far left.

There is an itch on the left side of my face, just in front of my ear.

A vehicle with a larger, heavier sound passes and a bit of jazz music makes an appearance much closer to my position. Only now do I realize I turned it on earlier at a quiet volume and it had been inaudible until this moment.

Someone arrives. I open my eyes. And it all goes away.

It's common to believe that life is a series of external experiences. And that we must live an outwardly extraordinary life in order to have something to share. The experience of our inner world is often completely overlooked.

If we focus on what's going on inside ourselves—sensations, emotions, the patterns of our thoughts—a wealth of material can be found. Our inner world is every bit as interesting, beautiful, and surprising as nature itself. It is, after all, born of nature.

When we go inside, we are processing what's going on outside. We're no longer separate. We're connected. We are one.

Ultimately, it doesn't make a difference whether your content originates on the inside or the outside. If a beautiful thought or phrase comes to mind, or if you see a beautiful sunset, one's not better than the other. Both are equally beautiful in different ways. It's helpful to consider there are always more options available to us than we might realize.

Memories and the Subconscious

When presented with new instrumental tracks for the first time, some vocalists record the first sounds out of their mouths, with no thought or preparation.

Often they'll sing random words or sounds that aren't words at all. It isn't uncommon, out of the gibberish, for a story to unfold or key phrases to appear.

There's no active attempt to write in this process. The work is being created on a subconscious level. The material exists hidden within.

There are practices that can assist in accessing this deeper well inside yourself. For example, you can try an anger-releasing exercise where you beat on a pillow for five minutes. It's more difficult than you might think to do this for the full duration. Time yourself and go hard. Then immediately fill five pages with whatever comes out.

The objective is to not think about it, to avoid directing the content in any way. Just write whatever words spill forth.

There's an abundant reservoir of high-quality information in our subconscious, and finding ways to access it can spark new material to draw from.

The psyche has admittance to a universal wisdom deeper than what we can come up with in our conscious mind. It provides a far less limited view. An oceanic source.

We don't know how it works and we don't know why it works, yet many artists tap into something beyond themselves without recognizing the process at play, purely through accessing the subconscious.

Often, reaching these states is outside of our control. Some artists have created their best works while feverish, with a temperature over 103. These trancelike conditions bypass the thinking part of the brain and access the dream state.

There's great wisdom in transitional realms between wakefulness and sleep. Right before you fall asleep, what thoughts and ideas come to you? How do you feel when you wake from a dream?

In the wisdom tradition of Tibetan dream yoga, among others, lamas say the dream state is just as real—or unreal—as the waking state.

Keeping a dream journal might be of use. Place a pen

and paper next to the bed, and as soon as you wake up, begin writing immediately with as much detail as possible before doing anything else. Try to limit any unnecessary movement. Simply turning your head can be enough to dislodge the dream from stored memory.

As you write, the picture will develop and you'll remember more of the story, more of the setting, more of the details than you did when you first set your pen to paper. The more you do this practice, morning after morning, the better you will get at recalling your dreams. It may also help to set an intention to remember your dreams before going to sleep.

Memories can also be thought of as dreamlike. They're more a romantic story than a faithful document of a life event. And there's good content to be found in these dreamy recollections we have of past experiences.

Another helpful tool is randomness—or, more accurately, apparent randomness, since there may be organization happening on a different level than we understand.

When we throw the I Ching, for example, we don't determine how the sticks or coins land. But through them, we get information we can use to help decision making, and once again bypass our conscious mind and perhaps tap into a larger intelligence.

It's Always There

(•)

I'm strongly affected by the sun. When it's a bright day, I feel energized. When it's gloomy, I'm gloomy.

On those overcast days, it helps to tune in to the fact that the sun is still there. It's just hidden behind a thicker layer of clouds. At noon, the sun is high in the sky, regardless of how light or dark it is outside.

In the same way, regardless of how much we're paying attention, the information we seek is out there. If we're aware, we get to tune in to more of it. If we're less aware, we miss it.

When we miss it, it really does pass us by. Tomorrow presents another opportunity for awareness, but it's never an opportunity for the same awareness.

Setting

(•)

We're affected by our surroundings, and finding the best environment to create a clear channel is personal and to be tested. It also depends on your intention.

Isolated places like a forest, a monastery, or a sailboat in the middle of the ocean are fine locations to receive direct transmissions from the universe.

If instead you want to tune in to the collective consciousness, you might sit in a busy spot with people coming and going and experience Source as filtered through humanity. This secondhand approach is no less valid.

One step further removed might be to plug into the culture itself, constantly consuming art, entertainment, news, and social media. All the while noticing the patterns the universe is promoting.

It's helpful to view currents in the culture without feeling obligated to follow the direction of their flow. Instead, notice them in the same connected, detached way you might notice a warm wind. Let yourself move within it, yet not be *of* it.

One person's connected place may be another's distraction. And different environments may be right at different points in your artistic process. Andy Warhol was said to create with a television, radio, and record player all on simultaneously. For Eminem, the noise of a single TV set is his preferred backdrop for writing. Marcel Proust lined his walls with sound-absorbing cork, closed the drapes, and wore earplugs. Kafka too took his need for silence to an extreme—"not like a hermit," he once said, but "like a dead man." There is no wrong way. There is only your way.

It's not always easy to follow the subtle energetic information the universe broadcasts, especially when your friends, family, coworkers, or those with a business interest in your creativity are offering seemingly rational advice that challenges your intuitive knowing. To the best of my ability, I've followed my intuition to make career turns, and been recommended against doing so every time. It helps to realize that it's better to follow the universe than those around you.

Interference may also come from the voices within. The ones in your head that murmur you're not talented enough, your idea isn't good enough, art isn't a worthwhile investment of your time, the result won't be well-received, you're a failure if the creation isn't successful. It's helpful to turn those voices down so you can hear the chimes of the cosmic clock ring, reminding you it's time.

Your time to participate.

Self-Doubt

(•)

Self-doubt lives in all of us. And while we may wish it gone, it is there to serve us.

Flaws are human, and the attraction of art is the humanity held in it. If we were machinelike, the art wouldn't resonate. It would be soulless. With life comes pain, insecurity, and fear.

We're all different and we're all imperfect, and the imperfections are what makes each of us and our work interesting. We create pieces reflective of who we are, and if insecurity is part of who we are, then our work will have a greater degree of truth in it as a result.

The making of art is not a competitive act. Our work is

representative of the self. You would be amiss to say, "I'm not up to the challenge." Yes, you may need to deepen your craft to fully realize your vision. If you're not up to it, no one else can do it. Only you can. You're the only one with your voice.

The people who choose to do art are, many times, the most vulnerable. There are singers considered among the best in the world who can't bring themselves to listen to their own voice. And these are not rare exceptions. Many artists in different arenas have similar issues.

The sensitivity that allows them to make the art is the same vulnerability that makes them more tender to being judged. Still, many continue to share their work and risk criticism in spite of this. It's as if they have no other choice. Being an artist is who they are, and they are made whole through self-expression.

If a creator is so afraid of judgment that they're unable to move forward, it might be that the desire to share the work isn't as strong as the desire to protect themselves. Perhaps art isn't their role. Their temperament might serve a different pursuit. This path is not for everyone. Adversity is part of the process.

We are not obligated to follow this calling because we have a talent or skill. It's worth remembering that we are blessed to get to create. It's a privilege. We're choosing it. We're not being ordered to do this. If we'd rather not do it, let's not do it.

Some successful artists are deeply insecure, self-sabotaging, struggling with addiction, or facing other obstacles to making and sharing their work. An unhealthy self-image or a hardship in life can fuel great art, creating a deep well of insight and emotion for an artist to draw from. They can also get in the way of the artist being able to make many things over a long period of time.

People who are particularly challenged in this sense generally can't produce creative work over and over again. This isn't because they're not artistically capable, but because they were only able to break through their own issues one or two times and share great work.

One of the reasons so many great artists die of overdoses early in their lives is because they're using drugs to numb a very painful existence. The reason it's painful is the reason they became artists in the first place: their incredible sensitivity.

If you see tremendous beauty or tremendous pain where other people see little or nothing at all, you're confronted with big feelings all the time. These emotions can be confusing and overwhelming. When those around you don't see what you see and feel what you feel, this can lead to a sense of isolation and a general feeling of not belonging, of otherness.

These charged emotions, powerful when expressed in the work, are the same dark clouds that beg to be numbed to allow sleep or to get out of bed and face the day in the morning. It's a blessing and a curse.

Make It Up

○

While the emotional undercurrents of self-doubt can serve the art, they can also interfere with the creative process. Beginning a work, completing a work, and sharing a work— these are key moments where many of us become stuck.

How do we move forward, considering the stories we tell ourselves?

One of the best strategies is to lower the stakes.

We tend to think that what we're making is the most important thing in our lives and that it's going to define us for all eternity. Consider moving forward with the more accurate point of view that it's a small work, a beginning. The mission is to complete the project so you can move on to the next. That next one is a stepping-stone to the following work. And so it continues in productive rhythm for the entirety of your creative life.

All art is a work in progress. It's helpful to see the piece we're working on as an experiment. One in which we can't predict the outcome. Whatever the result, we will receive useful information that will benefit the next experiment.

If you start from the position that there is no right or wrong, no good or bad, and creativity is just free play with no rules, it's easier to submerge yourself joyfully in the process of making things.

We're not playing to win, we're playing to play. And ultimately, playing is fun. Perfectionism gets in the way of fun. A more skillful goal might be to find comfort in the process. To make and put out successive works with ease.

Oscar Wilde said that some things are too important to be taken seriously. Art is one of those things. Setting the bar low, especially to get started, frees you to play, explore, and test without attachment to results.

This is not just a path to more supportive thoughts. Active play and experimentation until we're happily surprised is how the best work reveals itself.

⊙

Another approach to overcoming insecurities is to label them. I was working with an artist who was frozen by doubts and unable to move forward. I asked if he was familiar with the Buddhist concept of *papancha*, which translates as *preponderance of thoughts*. This speaks to the mind's tendency to respond to our experiences with an avalanche of mental chatter.

He responded, "I know exactly what that is. That's me."

Now that he had a name for what was holding him back, he was able to normalize his doubts and not take them so seriously. When they came up, we'd call them papancha, notice them, then move forward.

I was in a meeting with another artist who had just released a very successful album, but felt afraid to do more work and listed different reasons why she didn't want to make music anymore. There are always good reasons not to continue.

"It's fine, you don't have to make music ever again. There's nothing wrong with that. Just stop if it's not making you happy. It's your choice."

As soon as I said this, her expression changed and she realized she would be happier creating than not creating.

Gratitude can also help. Realizing you are fortunate to be in a position that allows you to create, and in some cases get paid to do what you love, might tip the balance in favor of the work.

Ultimately, your desire to create must be greater than your fear of it.

Even for some of the greatest artists, that fear never goes away. One legendary singer, despite performing for over five decades, was never able to eliminate his stage fright. Despite a terror so strong it made him sick to his stomach, he still stepped into the spotlight each night and performed a spellbinding show. By accepting self-doubt, rather than trying to eliminate or repress it, we lessen its energy and interference.

⊙

It's worth noting the distinction between doubting the work and doubting yourself. An example of doubting the work would be, "I don't know if my song is as good as it can be." Doubting yourself might sound like, "I can't write a good song."

These statements are worlds apart, both in accuracy and in impact on the nervous system. Doubting yourself can lead to a sense of hopelessness, of not being inherently fit to take on the task at hand. All or nothing thinking is a nonstarter.

However, doubting the quality of your work might, at times, help to improve it. You can doubt your way to excellence.

If you have an imperfect version of a work you really love, you may find that when it finally seems perfect, you don't love it in the same way. This is a sign the imperfect version was actually the one. The work is not about perfection.

One thing I learned through having spellcheck is that I regularly make up words. I'll type a word and then the computer will tell me it doesn't exist. Since it sounds like what

I'm aiming to say, I sometimes decide to use it anyway. I know what it means, and perhaps the reader will understand the meaning better than if I used an actual word.

The imperfections you're tempted to fix might prove to be what make the work great. And sometimes not. We rarely know what makes a piece great. No one can know. The most plausible reasons are theories at best. *Why* is beyond our comprehension.

The Leaning Tower of Pisa was an architectural error, which builders further exacerbated by trying to fix. Now, hundreds of years later, it's one of the most visited buildings in the world precisely because of this mistake.

In Japanese pottery, there's an artful form of repair called kintsugi. When a piece of ceramic pottery breaks, rather than trying to restore it to its original condition, the artisan accentuates the fault by using gold to fill the crack. This beautifully draws attention to where the work was broken, creating a golden vein. Instead of the flaw diminishing the work, it becomes a focal point, an area of both physical and aesthetic strength. The scar also tells the story of the piece, chronicling its past experience.

We can apply this same technique to ourselves and embrace our imperfections. Whatever insecurities we have can be reframed as a guiding force in our creativity. They only become a hindrance when they prevent our ability to share what's closest to our heart.

Art creates a profound connection
between the artist and the audience.
Through that connection,
both can heal.

Distraction

Distraction is one of the best tools available to the artist when used skillfully. In some cases, it's the only way to get where we are going.

When meditating, as soon as the mind quiets, the sense of space can be overtaken by a worry or a random thought. This is why many meditation schools teach students to use a mantra. An automatic, repeated phrase leaves little room in the mind for thoughts that pull us out of the moment.

The mantra, then, is a distraction. And while certain distractions can take you out of the present moment, others can keep the conscious part of yourself busy so that the unconscious is freed up to work for you. Worry beads, rosaries, and malas work in the same way.

When we reach an impasse at any point in the creative process, it can be helpful to step away from the project to create space and allow a solution to appear.

We might hold a problem to be solved lightly in the back of our consciousness instead of the front of our mind. This way, we can remain present with it over time while engaging in a simple, unrelated task. Examples include driving, walking, swimming, showering, washing dishes, dancing, or performing any activity we can accomplish on autopilot. At times, physical movement can spur ideas to move too.

Some musicians, for example, do a better job of writing melodies while driving than sitting in a room with an audio recorder on. These types of distractions keep one part of the mind busy while freeing the rest to remain open to whatever comes in. Perhaps this process of *nonthinking thought* allows us to access a different part of our brain. One that can see more angles than the direct path.

Distraction is not procrastination. Procrastination consistently undermines our ability to make things. Distraction is a strategy in service of the work.

Sometimes disengaging
is the best way to engage.

Collaboration

(•)

Nothing begins with us.

The more we pay attention, the more we begin to realize that all the work we ever do is a collaboration.

It's a collaboration with the art that's come before you and the art that will come after. It's also a collaboration with the world you're living in. With the experiences you've had. With the tools you use. With the audience. And with who you are today.

The "self" has many distinct aspects. It's possible to create a piece, love it, and then look at it the next day and feel completely different about it. The inspired-artist aspect of your self may be in conflict with the craftsperson aspect, disappointed that the craftsperson is unable to create the physical embodiment of the inspired artist's vision. This is a common conflict for creators, since there is no direct conversion from abstract thought to the material world. The work is always an interpretation.

There are many different hats the artist wears, and creativity is an internal discussion between these aspects of self. The negotiation continues until the selves create the best work they can together.

The work itself also wears different hats. You may make a piece and feel you know exactly what it is, then someone else may experience it and sense they know what it is, and yet what you see and what they see may be completely different. What's of particular interest about this is that neither one is right. And both are right.

This is not something to be concerned about. If the artist is happy with the work they're creating and the viewer is enlivened by the work they're experiencing, it doesn't matter if they see it in the same way. In fact, it is impossible for anyone to experience your work as you do, or as anyone else does.

You could have a distinct idea of what a piece means, how it functions, or why it's pleasing—and someone else can like it or dislike it for an entirely different reason.

The purpose of the work is to awaken something in you first, and then allow something to be awakened in others. And it's fine if they're not the same thing. We can only hope that the *magnitude* of the charge we experience reverberates as powerfully for others as it does for us.

Sometimes the artist may not be the crafter of the work. Marcel Duchamp would find everyday objects—a snow shovel, a bicycle wheel, a urinal—and simply decide they were art. He called them readymades. A painting is just a painting until you put a frame on it and hang it on the wall, then it's called art.

What's considered art is simply an agreement. And none of it is true.

What is true is that you are never alone when you're making art. You are in a constant dialogue with what is and what was, and the closer you can tune in to that discussion, the better you can serve the work before you.

Intention

An old man in Calcutta would walk to get water from a well every day. He'd carry a clay pot and lower it by hand slowly, all the way down, careful not to let it hit the sides of the well and break.

Once it was full, he'd raise the pot slowly and carefully again. It was a focused, time-consuming act.

One day, a traveler noticed the old man engaged in this difficult task. More experienced with mechanics, he showed the old man how to use a pulley system.

"This will allow the pot to go straight down quickly," the traveler explained, "then fill with water and come back up, without hitting the sides. It's much easier and the pot will be just as full with much less work."

The old man looked at him and said, "I think I'm going to keep doing it the way I always have. I really have to think about each movement and there's a great deal of care that goes into doing it right. I'd imagine if I were to use the pulley, it would become easy and I might even start thinking about something else while doing it. If I put so little care and time into it, what might the water taste like? It couldn't possibly taste as good."

Our thoughts, feelings, processes, and unconscious beliefs have an energy that is hidden in the work. This unseen, un-measurable force gives each piece its magnetism. A com-pleted project is only made up of our intention and our experiments around it. Remove intention and all that's left is the ornamental shell.

Though the artist may have a number of goals and moti-vations, there is only one intention. This is the grand gesture of the work.

It is not an exercise of thought, a goal to be set, or a means of commodification. It is a truth that lives inside you. Through your living it, that truth becomes embedded in the work. If the work doesn't represent who you are and what you're liv-ing, how can it hold an energetic charge?

An intention is more than a conscious purpose, it's the

congruence of that purpose. It requires an alignment of all aspects of one's self. Of conscious thought and unconscious beliefs, of capabilities and commitment, of actions when working and not. It's a state of living in harmonic agreement with oneself.

Not all projects take time, but they do take a lifetime. In calligraphy, the work is created in one movement of the brush. All the intention is in that single concentrated movement. The line is a reflection of the energy transfer from the artist's being, including the entire history of their experiences, thoughts, and apprehensions, into the hand. The creative energy exists in the journey to the making, not in the act of constructing.

⊙

Our work embodies a higher purpose. Whether we know it or not, we're a conduit for the universe. Material is allowed through us. If we are a clear channel, our intention reflects the intention of the cosmos.

Most creators think of themselves as the conductor of the orchestra. If we zoom out of our small view of reality, we function more as an instrumentalist in a much larger symphony the universe is orchestrating.

We may not have a great understanding of what this magnum opus is because we only see the small part we play.

The bee, attracted by the scent of the flower, lands on one

then another, inadvertently enabling reproduction. Should the bee go extinct, not just flowers but birds, small mammals, and humans would likely also cease to exist. It's fair to assume that the bee doesn't know its role in this interconnected puzzle and in preserving the balance of nature. The bee is simply being.

Similarly, the total output of human creativity, in all its kaleidoscopic breadth, pieces together the fabric forming our culture. The underlying intention of our work is the aspect allowing it to fit neatly into this fabric. Rarely if ever do we know the grand intention, yet if we surrender to the creative impulse, our singular piece of the puzzle takes its proper shape.

Intention is all there is. The work is just a reminder.

Rules

A rule is any guiding principle or creative criterion. It might exist within the artist, the genre, or the culture. Rules, by their nature, are limitations.

The laws of math and science are different from the rules we are looking at here. Those laws describe precise relationships in the physical world, which we know to be true by testing them against the world itself.

The rules artists learn are different. They are assumptions, not absolutes. They describe a goal or method for short-term or long-term results. They are there to be tested. And they are only of value as long as they are helpful. They are not laws of nature.

All kinds of assumptions masquerade as laws: a suggestion from a self-help book, something heard in an interview, your favorite artist's best tip, an expression in the culture, or something a teacher once told you.

Rules direct us to average behaviors. If we're aiming to create works that are exceptional, most rules don't apply. Average is nothing to aspire to.

The goal is not to fit in. If anything, it's to amplify the differences, what doesn't fit, the special characteristics unique to how you see the world.

Instead of sounding like others, value your own voice. Develop it. Cherish it.

As soon as a convention is established, the most interesting work would likely be the one that doesn't follow it. The reason to make art is to innovate and self-express, show something new, share what's inside, and communicate your singular perspective.

⊙

Pressures and expectations come from different directions. Society's mores dictate what's right and wrong, what's accepted and frowned upon, what's celebrated and reviled.

The artists who define each generation are generally the ones who live outside of these boundaries. Not the artists who embody the beliefs and conventions of their time, but the ones who transcend them. Art is confrontation. It widens the audience's reality, allowing them to glimpse life through a different window. One with the potential for a glorious new view.

In the beginning, we approach our craft with a template of what's come before. If you're writing a song, you might think it should be three to five minutes long and have a certain amount of repetition.

To a bird, a song is a very different thing. The bird doesn't prefer a three-to-five-minute format or accept the chorus as the hook, yet the song for the bird is just as sonorous. And even more intrinsic to the bird's being. It's an invitation, a warning, a way to connect, a means of survival.

It's a healthy practice to approach our work with as few accepted rules, starting points, and limitations as possible. Often the standards in our chosen medium are so ubiquitous, we take them for granted. They are invisible and unquestioned. This makes it nearly impossible to think outside the standard paradigm.

Visit an art museum. Most of the paintings you'll see are canvas stretched over a rectangular frame made of wood, whether it's Jacques-Louis David's *The Death of Socrates* or the Altarpiece paintings of Hilma af Klint. The content may vary yet the materials are consistent. There's a generally accepted standard.

If you want to paint, you're likely to begin by stretching canvas over a rectangular wooden frame and propping it up on an easel. Based solely on the tools selected, you've already exponentially narrowed what's possible, before a single drop of paint has made contact with the canvas.

We assume the equipment and format are part of the art form itself. Yet painting can be anything that involves the use of color on a surface for an aesthetic or communicative purpose. All other decisions are up to the artist.

Similar conventions are woven into most art forms: a book is a certain number of pages and is divided into chapters. A feature film is 90 to 120 minutes and often has three acts. Embedded in each medium, there are sets of norms that restrain our work before we've even begun.

Genres, in particular, come with distinct variations on rules. A horror film, a ballet, or a country album—each come with specific expectations. As soon as you use a label to describe what you're working on, there's a temptation to conform to its rules.

The templates of the past can be an inspiration in the beginning phases, but it's helpful to think beyond what's been done before. The world isn't waiting for more of the same.

Often, the most innovative ideas come from those who master the rules to such a degree that they can see past them or from those who never learned them at all.

⊙

The most deceptive rules are not the ones we can see, but the ones we can't. These can be found hiding deeper in the mind, often unnoticed, just beyond our awareness. Rules that entered our thinking through childhood programming, lessons we've forgotten, osmosis from the culture, and emulating the artists who inspired us to try it for ourselves.

These rules can serve or limit us. Be aware of any assumptions based on conventional wisdom.

Rules obeyed unconsciously are far stronger than the ones set on purpose. And they are more likely to undermine the work.

⊙

Every innovation risks becoming a rule. And innovation risks becoming an end in itself.

When we make a discovery that serves our work, it's not unusual to concretize this into a formula. On occasion, we decide this formula is who we are as an artist. What our voice is and isn't.

While this may benefit certain makers, it can be a limitation for others. Sometimes a formula has diminishing returns. Other times, we don't recognize that the formula is only a small aspect of what gives the work its charge.

It's helpful to continually challenge your own process. If you had a good result using a specific style, method, or working condition, don't assume that is the best way. Or your way. Or the only way. Avoid getting religious about it. There may be other strategies that work just as well and allow new possibilities, directions, and opportunities.

This is not always true, but it's something to consider.

⊙

Holding every rule as breakable is a healthy way to live as an artist. It loosens constraints that promote a predictable sameness in our working methods.

As you get further along in your career, a consistency may develop that's of less interest over time. Your work can start to feel like a job or a responsibility. So it's helpful to notice if you've been working with the same palette of colors all along.

Start the next project by scrapping that palette. The uncertainty that results can be a thrilling and scary proposition. Once you have a new framework, some elements of your older process may find their way back into the work, and that's okay.

It's helpful to remember that when you throw away an old playbook, you still get to keep the skills you learned along the way. These hard-earned abilities transcend rules. They're yours to keep. Imagine what can arise when you overlay an entirely new set of materials and instructions over your accumulated expertise.

As you move away from familiar rules, you may bump up against more hidden rules that have been guiding you all along, without your knowledge. Once recognized, these rules may be released or used with more intention.

Any rule is worth testing, be it conscious or unconscious. Challenge your assumptions and methods. You might find a better way. And even if it's not better, you'll learn from the experience. All of these experiments are like free throws. You have nothing to lose.

Beware of the assumption
that the way you work
is the best way
simply because
it's the way you've done it before.

The Opposite Is True

For any rules you accept

of what you can and cannot do as an artist . . .

of what your voice is and isn't . . .

of what's required to do the work and what you don't need . . .

it would be worthwhile to try the opposite.

If you're a sculptor, for example, you might start with the idea that what you're making has to exist in the material world. That would be a rule.

To explore the opposite would be to consider how a sculpture can exist without being a physical object. Perhaps your best work could be conceived digitally or conceptually, with no solid footprint. Or maybe it won't be your best work, but the thought process might lead you somewhere novel and intriguing.

Think of a rule as an imbalance. Darkness and light are only meaningful in relationship with each other. Without one, the other wouldn't exist. They are a matched dynamic system, like yin and yang.

Examine your methods and consider what the opposite would be. What would balance the scales? What would be the light to your dark, or the dark to your light? It's not uncommon for an artist to focus on one end of the seesaw. Even if we don't choose to create on the other side, understanding this polarity can inform our choices.

Another strategy might be to double down, to take the shades you're currently working in to the extreme.

Only through experimenting with balance do you discover where you are on the seesaw. Once you identify your position, you can move to the opposite side to find balance or go further out along the limb you're on, creating more leverage.

For every rule followed, examine the possibility that the opposite might be similarly interesting. Not necessarily better, just different. In the same way, you can try the opposite or the extreme of what's suggested in these pages and it will likely be just as fruitful.

Listening

When listening, there is only now. In Buddhist practice, a bell is rung as part of the ritual. The sound instantly pulls the participant into the present moment. It's a small reminder to wake up.

While the eyes and the mouth can be sealed, an ear has no lid, nothing to close. It takes in what surrounds it. It receives but can't transmit.

The ear is simply present to the world.

When we hear, sounds enter the ear autonomously. Often, we're not aware of all the individual sounds and their full range.

Listening is paying attention to those sounds, being

present with them, being in communion with them. Though to say that we listen with the ears, or the mind, might be a misconception. We listen with the whole body, our whole self.

The vibrations filling the space around us, the act of sound waves hitting the body, the spatial perceptions they indicate, the internal physical reactions they stimulate—this is all part of listening. Certain bass sounds can be felt only in the body, they can't be perceived by the ears.

The difference can be noticed when listening to music through headphones instead of speakers.

Headphones create an illusion, tricking your senses into believing you are hearing everything the music is offering. Many artists refuse to use headphones in the studio as it is a poor replica of the real-world listening experience. With speakers, we are closer to the sound of instruments in the room—immersed physically in a full sonic spectrum of vibration.

Many of us experience life as if we're taking it in through a pair of headphones. We strip away the full register. We hear information, but don't detect the subtler vibrations of feeling in the body.

When you practice listening with the whole self, you expand the scope of your consciousness to include vast amounts of information otherwise missed, and discover more material to feed your art habit.

If it's music you're listening to, consider closing your eyes.

You may find yourself getting lost in the experience. When the piece ends, you might be surprised by where you find yourself. You've been transported to another place. The place where the music lives.

⊙

Communication moves in two directions, even when one person speaks and another listens silently.

When the listener is totally present, the speaker often communicates differently. Most people aren't used to being fully heard, and it can be jarring for them.

Sometimes we block the flow of information being offered and compromise true listening. Our critical mind may kick in, taking note of what we agree with and what we don't, or what we like and dislike. We may look for reasons to distrust the speaker or make them wrong.

Formulating an opinion is not listening. Neither is preparing a response, or defending our position or attacking another's. To listen impatiently is to hear nothing at all.

Listening is suspending disbelief.

We are openly receiving. Paying attention with no preconceived ideas. The only goal is to fully and clearly understand what is being transmitted, remaining totally present with what's being expressed—and allowing it to be what it is.

Anything less is not only a disservice to the speaker, but also to yourself. While creating and defending a story in your own head, you miss information that might alter or evolve your current thoughts.

If we can go beyond our reflexive response, we may find there is something more beneath that resonates with us or helps our understanding. The new information might reinforce an idea, slightly alter it, or completely reverse it.

Listening without prejudice is how we grow and learn as people. More often than not, there are no right answers, just different perspectives. The more perspectives we can learn to see, the greater our understanding becomes. Our filter can begin to more accurately approach what truly is, rather than a narrow sliver interpreted through our bias.

Regardless of the type of art you're making, listening opens possibilities. It allows you to see a bigger world. Many of our beliefs were learned before we had a choice in what we were taught. Some of them might go back generations and may no longer apply. Some may never have applied.

Listening, then, is not just awareness. It's freedom from accepted limitations.

Patience

●

There are no shortcuts.

The lottery winner isn't ultimately happy after their sudden change of fortune. The home built hastily rarely survives the first storm. The single-sentence summary of a book or news event is no substitute for the full story.

We often take shortcuts without knowing it. When listening, we tend to skip forward and generalize the speaker's overall message. We miss the subtleties of the point, if not the entire premise. In addition to the assumption that we are saving time, this shortcut also avoids the discomfort of challenging our prevailing stories. And our worldview continues to shrink.

The artist actively works to experience life slowly, and then to re-experience the same thing anew. To read slowly, and to read and read again.

I might read a paragraph that inspires a thought, and while my eyes continue moving across the page in the physical act of reading, my mind may still be lost in the previous idea. I'm not taking in information anymore. When I realize this, I return to the last paragraph I can recall and start reading from there again. Sometimes it's three or four pages back.

Re-reading even a well-understood paragraph or page can be revelatory. New meanings, deeper understandings, inspirations, and nuances arise and come into focus.

Reading, in addition to listening, eating, and most physical activities, can be experienced like driving: we can participate either on autopilot or with focused intention. So often we sleepwalk through our lives. Consider how different your experience of the world might be if you engaged in every activity with the attention you might give to landing a plane.

There are those who approach the opportunities of each day like crossing items off a to-do list instead of truly engaging and participating with all of themselves.

Our continual quest for efficiency discourages looking too deeply. The pressure to deliver doesn't grant us time to consider all possibilities. Yet it's through deliberate action and repetition that we gain deeper insight.

⊙

Patience is required for the
nuanced development of your craft.

Patience is required for taking in
information in the most faithful way possible.

Patience is required for crafting a work that
resonates and contains all that we have to offer.

Every phase of an artist's work and life benefits from cultivating this achievable habit.

Patience is developed much like awareness. Through an acceptance of what is. Impatience is an argument with reality. The desire for something to be different from what we are experiencing in the here and now. A wish for time to speed up, tomorrow to come sooner, to relive yesterday, or to close your eyes then open them and find yourself in another place.

Time is something that we have no control over. So patience begins with acceptance of natural rhythms. The implied benefit of impatience is to save time by speeding up and skipping ahead of those rhythms. Paradoxically, this ends up taking more time and using more energy. It's wasted effort.

When it comes to the creative process, patience is accepting that the majority of the work we do is out of our control.

We can't force greatness to happen. All we can do is invite it in and await it actively. Not anxiously, as this might scare it off. Simply in a state of continual welcoming.

If we remove time from the equation of a work's development, what we're left with is patience. Not just for the development of the work, but for the development of the artist as a whole. Even the masterpieces that have been produced on tight timelines are the sum of decades spent patiently laboring on other works.

If there is a rule to creativity that's less breakable than the others, it's that the need for patience is ever-present.

Beginner's Mind

(•)

Some three thousand years ago in China, the strategic board game Go was developed. Some believe warlords and generals based it on the stones they'd place on maps to determine their battle plans. Besides being the oldest continually played board game in human history, it's also one of the most complex.

In modern times, beating this game became known in the artificial intelligence community as the holy grail. Since the number of possible configurations on the board is larger than the number of atoms in the universe, it was believed computers didn't have the processing power needed to beat a skilled human player.

Rising to the challenge, scientists built an artificial intelligence program called AlphaGo. The program learned to play by teaching itself, studying more than 100,000 past games. It then played against itself over and over until it was ready to challenge the reigning grandmaster of the game.

In move 37 of the second match, the machine was faced with a decision that would determine the way the rest of the game would be played. There were two apparent choices to be made. Choice A was the kind of move that would signal the computer was playing a game of offense. Choice B would signal it was playing a defensive game.

Instead, the computer decided to make a third move, a move no one steeped in the game had ever made in thousands of years of play. "Not a single human player would choose move 37," one commentator said. Most thought it was a mistake or simply a bad move.

The grandmaster playing against the machine was so taken aback, he stood up and walked out of the room. He eventually returned, not with his usual confident composure but visibly shaken and frustrated by the experience. In the end, AlphaGo won the game. And that never-been-seen-before move, experts said, was the one that turned the course of the game in favor of the AI.

In the end, the computer won four out of five matches, and the grandmaster permanently retired from competition.

⊙

Upon first hearing this story, I found myself in tears, and confused by this sudden swell of emotion. After further reflection, I realized that the story spoke to the power of purity in the creative act.

What was it that allowed a machine to devise a move no one steeped in the game had ever made in thousands of years of play?

It wasn't necessarily its intelligence. It was the fact that the machine learned the game from scratch, with no coach, no human intervention, no lessons based on an expert's past experience. The AI followed the fixed rules, not the millennia of accepted cultural norms attached to them. It didn't take into account the three-thousand-year-old traditions and conventions of Go. It didn't accept the narrative of how to properly play this game. It wasn't held back by limiting beliefs.

And so this wasn't just a landmark event in AI development. It was the first time Go had been played with the full spectrum of possibilities available. With a clean slate, Alpha-Go was able to innovate, devise something completely new, and transform the game forever. If it had been taught to play by humans, it most likely wouldn't have won the tournament.

One Go expert commented, "After humanity spent thousands of years improving our tactics, computers tell us that humans are completely wrong . . . I would go as far as to say not a single human has touched the edge of the truth of Go."

To see what no human has seen before, to know what no human has known before, to create as no human has created before, it may be necessary to see as if through eyes that have never seen, know through a mind that has never thought, create with hands that have never been trained.

This is beginner's mind—one of the most difficult states of being to dwell in for an artist, precisely because it involves letting go of what our experiences have taught us.

Beginner's mind is starting from a pure childlike place of not knowing. Living in the moment with as few fixed beliefs as possible. Seeing things for what they are as presented. Tuning in to what enlivens us in the moment instead of what we think will work. And making our decisions accordingly. Any preconceived ideas and accepted conventions limit what's possible.

We tend to believe that the more we know, the more clearly we can see the possibilities available. This is not the case. The impossible only becomes accessible when experience has not taught us limits. Did the computer win because it knew more than the grandmaster or because it knew less?

There's a great power in not knowing. When faced with a challenging task, we may tell ourselves it's too difficult, it's not worth the effort, it's not the way things are done, it's not likely to work, or it's not likely to work *for us*.

If we approach a task with ignorance, it can remove the barricade of knowledge blocking progress. Curiously, not being aware of a challenge may be just what we need to rise to it.

⊙

Innocence brings forth innovation. A lack of knowledge can create more openings to break new ground. The Ramones thought they were making mainstream bubblegum pop. To most others, the lyrical content alone—about lobotomies, sniffing glue, and pinheads—was enough to challenge this assumption.

While the band saw themselves as the next Bay City Rollers, they unwittingly invented punk rock and started a countercultural revolution. While the music of the Bay City Rollers had great success in its time, the Ramones' singular take on rock and roll became more popular and influential. Of all the explanations of the Ramones, the most apt may be: innovation through ignorance.

⊙

Experience provides wisdom to draw from, but it tempers the power of naivete. The past can be a teacher, offering tried and true methods, familiarity with the standards of the craft, awareness of potential risks, and in some cases virtuosity. It lures us into a pattern that absolves us of the opportunity to engage innocently with the task at hand.

The more ingrained your adopted approach, the harder it is to see past it. Though experience doesn't rule out innovation, it can make it more difficult to access.

Animals, like children, don't have a hard time making a decision. They act out of innate instinct, not learned behavior. This primitive force packs an ancient wisdom that science has yet to catch up with.

These childlike superpowers include being in the moment, valuing play above all else, having no regard for consequences, being radically honest without consideration, and having the ability to freely move from one emotion to the next without holding on to story. For children, each moment in time is all there is. No future, no past. *I want it now, I'm hungry, I'm tired.* All pure authenticity.

The great artists throughout history are the ones able to maintain this childlike enthusiasm and exuberance naturally. Just as an infant is selfish, they're protective of their art in a way that's not always cooperative. Their needs as a creator come first. Often at the expense of their personal lives and relationships.

For one of the most loved singer-songwriters of all time, if inspiration comes through, it takes precedence over other obligations. His friends and family understand that in the middle of a meal, conversation, or event, if a song calls, he'll exit the scene and tend to it, without explanation.

Accessing childlike spirit in our art and our lives is worth aspiring to. It's simple to do if you haven't accumulated too many fixed habits and thoughts. If you have, it's very difficult. Nearly impossible.

A child has no set of premises it relies on to make sense of the world. It may serve you to do the same. Any label you assume before sitting down to create, even one as foundational as sculptor, rapper, author, or entrepreneur, could be doing more harm than good. Strip away the labels. Now how do you see the world?

Try to experience everything as if for the first time. If you grew up in a landlocked town that you never left, the first time you traveled and saw the ocean would likely be a dramatic, awe-inspiring experience. If you spent your whole life living near the ocean, your experience of it would almost certainly be less dramatic.

When you see what's present around you as if for the first time, you start to realize how astonishing it all is.

As artists, we aim to live in a way in which we see the extraordinary hidden in the seemingly mundane. Then challenge ourselves to share what we see in a way that allows others a glimpse of this remarkable beauty.

Talent is the ability to let ideas
manifest themselves through you.

Inspiration

It appears in a moment.

An immaculate conception.

A divine flash of light. An idea that would otherwise require labor to unfold suddenly blooms in a single inhalation.

What defines inspiration is the quality and quantity of the download. At a speed so instantaneous, it seems impossible to process. Inspiration is the rocket fuel powering our work. It is a universal conversation we yearn to be part of.

The word comes from the Latin—*inspirare*, meaning to breathe in or blow into.

For the lungs to draw in air, they must first be emptied.

For the mind to draw inspiration, it wants space to welcome the new. The universe seeks balance. Through this absence, you are inviting energy in.

The same principle applies to everything in life. If we are looking for a relationship when we're already in one, then we are full. There is no room for the new to enter. And we are unable to welcome in the relationship we want.

To create space for inspiration, we might consider practices of quieting the mind: meditation, awareness, silence, contemplation, prayer, any ritual that helps us fend off distraction and papancha.

Breath itself is a potent vehicle to calm our thoughts, create space, and tune in. It cannot guarantee that inspiration will come, though the vacancy may draw the muse in to play.

Taken more spiritually, inspiration means *to breathe life into*. An ancient interpretation defines it as the immediate influence of the divine. For the artist, inspiration is a breath of creative force drawn in instantly from outside of our small selves. We can't be sure where this spark of insight originates. It's helpful to know it's not us alone.

When inspiration does arrive, it is invariably energizing. But it is not something to rely on. An artistic life cannot be built solely around waiting. Inspiration is out of our control and can prove hard to find. Effort is required and invitations are to be extended. In its absence, we may work on other areas of the project independent of this cosmic transmission.

Epiphanies are hidden in the most ordinary of moments: the casting of a shadow, the smell of a match igniting, an unusual phrase overheard or misheard. A dedication to the practice of showing up on a regular basis is the main requirement.

To vary your inspiration, consider varying your inputs. Turn the sound off to watch a film, listen to the same song on repeat, read only the first word of each sentence in a short story, arrange stones by size or color, learn to lucid dream.

Break habits.

Look for differences.

Notice connections.

One indicator of inspiration is awe. We tend to take so much for granted. How can we move past disconnection and desensitization to the incredible wonders of nature and human engineering all around us?

Most of what we see in the world holds the potential to inspire astonishment if looked at from a less jaded perspective. Train yourself to see the awe behind the obvious. Look at the world from this vantage point as often as possible. Submerge yourself.

The beauty around us enriches our lives in so many ways. It is an end in itself. And it sets an example for our own work. We can aim to develop an eye for harmony and balance, as if our creations have always been here, like mountains or feathers.

Ride the wave as long as it can be ridden. If you are fortunate enough to experience the strike of inspiration, take full advantage of the access. Remain in the energy of this rarefied moment for as long as it lasts. When flowing, keep going.

If you're a writer and you tap into a stream of ideas before bed, you may want to stay with it until dawn. If you're a musician and you've reached your goal of creating one song or ten songs, yet the music is still coming, capture all you can.

The work yielded may not be used in the current project, but it may be of use another time. Or it may not. The task of the artist is simply to recognize the transmission and stay with it in gratitude, until it truly runs its course.

In terms of priority, inspiration comes first. You come next. The audience comes last.

These are special moments and are to be treated with the utmost devotion. Our schedules are set aside when these fleeting moments of illumination come. Summon your strength and commit yourself on behalf of this offering, even when it arises at an inopportune time. This is the serious artist's obligation.

John Lennon once advised that if you start a song, write it through to the end in that sitting. The initial inspiration has a vitality in it that can carry you through the whole piece. Don't be concerned if some of the parts are not yet all they can be. Get through a rough draft. A full, imperfect version is generally more helpful than a seemingly perfect fragment.

When an idea forms, or a hook is written, we may feel that we've cracked the code and the rest will take care of itself. If we step away and let that initial spark fade, we may return to find it's not so easy to rekindle. Think of inspiration as a force not immune to the laws of entropy.

Habits

The first thing I would show players at our initial day of training was how to take a little extra time putting on their shoes and socks properly.

The most important part of your equipment is your shoes and socks. You play on a hard floor. So you must have shoes that fit right. And you must not permit your socks to have wrinkles around the little toe—where you generally get blisters—or around the heels.

I showed my players how I wanted them to do it. Hold up the sock, work it around the little toe area and the heel area so that there are no wrinkles.

Smooth it out good. Then hold the sock up while you put the shoe on. And the shoe must be spread apart— not just pulled on the top laces.

You tighten it up snugly by each eyelet. Then you tie it. And then you double-tie it so it won't come undone—because I don't want shoes coming untied during practice, or during the game. I don't want that to happen.

That's just a little detail that coaches must take advantage of, because it's the little details that make the big things come about.

The sentiments above are John Wooden's, the most successful coach in the history of college basketball. His teams won more consecutive games and championships than any others in history.

It must have been frustrating for these elite athletes, who wanted to get on the court and show what they could do, to arrive at practice for the first time with this legendary coach only to hear him say, Today we will learn to tie our shoes.

The point Wooden was making was that creating effective habits, down to the smallest detail, is what makes the difference between winning and losing games. Each habit might seem small, but added together, they have an exponential effect on performance. Just one habit, at the top of any field, can be enough to give an edge over the competition.

Wooden considered every aspect of the game where an issue might arise, and trained his players for each one. Repeatedly. Until they became habits.

The goal was immaculate performance. Wooden often said the only person you're ever competing against is yourself. The rest is out of your control.

This way of thinking applies to the creative life just as well. For both the artist and the athlete, the details matter, whether the players recognize their importance or not.

Good habits create good art. The way we do anything is the way we do everything. Treat each choice you make, each action you take, each word you speak with skillful care. The goal is to live your life in the service of art.

⊙

Consider establishing a consistent framework around your creative process. It is often the case that the more set in your personal regimen, the more freedom you have within that structure to express yourself.

Discipline and freedom seem like opposites. In reality, they are partners. Discipline is not a lack of freedom, it is a harmonious relationship with time. Managing your schedule and daily habits well is a necessary component to free up the practical and creative capacity to make great art.

It could even be said that a focused efficiency in life is more important than one in work. Approaching the practical aspects of your day with military precision allows the artistic windows to be opened in childlike freedom.

Creativity-supporting habits can begin the moment you arise each day. These might include looking at sunlight before screenlight, meditating (outdoors if possible), exercising, and showering in cold water before beginning creative time in a suitable space.

These habits look different for everyone, and perhaps different for the same artist from day to day. You might sit in the forest, pay attention to your thoughts, and make notes. Or drive in a car for an hour, with no destination in mind, listening to classical music and seeing if any sparks arise.

It's helpful to set scheduled office hours, or uninterrupted periods of joyful play that allow your imagination to soar. For one person, that window of time might be three hours, for another thirty minutes. Some prefer to work from dusk 'til dawn, while others create in twenty-minute sessions, with five-minute breaks between each.

Find the sustainable rituals that best support your work. If you set a routine that is oppressive, you'll likely find excuses not to show up. It's in the interest of your art to create an easily achievable schedule to start with.

If you commit to working for half an hour a day, something good can happen that generates momentum. You may then look at the clock and realize you've been working for two hours. The option is always open to extend your creative hours once the habit is formed.

Feel free to experiment. The goal is to commit to a structure that can take on a life of its own, instead of creating only when the mood strikes. Or to start each day with the question of how and when you're going to work on your art.

Put the decision making into the work, not into *when* to work. The more you reduce your daily life-maintenance tasks, the greater the bandwidth available for creative decisions. Albert Einstein wore the same thing daily: a gray suit. Erik Satie had seven identical outfits, one for each day of the week. Limit your practical choices to free your creative imagination.

⊙

We all yearn to establish new healthy, productive habits, such as exercising, eating more local, natural foods, or practicing our craft more regularly.

But how often do we consider examining and removing the habits that currently drive our days? How often do we regard behaviors accepted as "the way people are" or "the way we are" merely as habits?

Each of us has automatic habits. We have habits in movement. Habits in speech, thought, and perception. Habits in being ourselves. Some of them have been practiced every day since we were children. A pathway gets carved into the brain and becomes difficult to change. Most of these habits control us, beyond our decisions, to the point they function autonomously and automatically, like the regulation of our body temperature.

I recently learned a different way of swimming. It felt awkward and counterintuitive, because I learned to swim when I was very young. My previous method was so ingrained, I didn't ever have to think about it. I effortlessly knew how to do it. It had worked well enough to get me from one side of the pool to the other, even though there were other ways that could take me farther and faster with more ease.

In our artistic pursuits, we also rely on habits to get from one point to another. Some of them don't serve the work or they undermine its progress. When we stay open and pay close attention, it is possible to recognize these less helpful habits and soften their spell. And begin to explore new practices. Ones that come in and out of our creative lives like temporary collaborators, remaining as long as they serve the work and departing when they are no longer beneficial.

Thoughts and habits not conducive to the work:

- Believing you're not good enough.

- Feeling you don't have the energy it takes.

- Mistaking adopted rules for absolute truths.

- Not wanting to do the work (laziness).

- Not taking the work to its highest expression (settling).

- Having goals so ambitious that you can't begin.

- Thinking you can only do your best work in certain conditions.

- Requiring specific tools or equipment to do the work.

- Abandoning a project as soon as it gets difficult.

- Feeling like you need permission to start or move forward.

- Letting a perceived need for funding, equipment, or support get in the way.

- Having too many ideas and not knowing where to start.

- Never finishing projects.

- Blaming circumstances or other people for interfering with your process.

- Romanticizing negative behaviors or addictions.

- Believing a certain mood or state is necessary to do your best work.

- Prioritizing other activities and responsibilities over your commitment to making art.

- Distractibility and procrastination.

- Impatience.

- Thinking anything that's out of your control is in your way.

Create an environment
where you're free to express
what you're afraid to express.

Seeds

In the first phase of the creative process, we are to be completely open, collecting anything we find of interest.

We can call this the Seed phase. We're searching for potential starting points that, with love and care, can grow into something beautiful. At this stage, we are not comparing them to find the best seed. We simply gather them.

A seed for a song could be a phrase, a melody, a bass line, or a rhythmic feel.

For a written piece, it may be a sentence, a character sketch, a setting, a thesis, or a plot point.

For a structure, a shape, a material choice, a function, or the natural properties of a location.

And for a business, it could be a common inconvenience, a societal need, a technical advancement, or a personal interest.

Collecting seeds typically doesn't involve a tremendous amount of effort. It's more a receiving of a transmission. A noticing.

As if catching fish, we walk to the water, bait the hook, cast the line, and patiently wait. We cannot control the fish, only the presence of our line.

The artist casts a line to the universe. We don't get to choose when a noticing or inspiration comes. We can only be there to receive it. As with meditation, our engagement in the process is what allows the result.

Collecting seeds is best approached with active awareness and boundless curiosity. It cannot be muscled, though perhaps it can be willed.

⊙

As the seeds arrive, forming conclusions about their value or fate can get in the way of their natural potential. In this phase, the artist's work is to collect seeds, plant them, water them with attention, and see if they take root.

Having a specific vision of what a seed will become could serve as a helpful guide in later phases. In this initial stage, it may cut off more interesting possibilities.

An idea appearing to hold less vitality may grow into a

beautiful work. Other times, the most exciting seed may not ultimately yield fruit. It's too soon to tell. Until we are further along in the process and the idea has been developed, it's impossible to assess these germs of an idea accurately. The appropriate seed will reveal itself over time.

Placing too much emphasis on a seed or dismissing it prematurely can interfere with its natural growth. The temptation to insert too much of yourself in this first phase can undermine the entire enterprise. Be wary of taking shortcuts or crossing items off your list too quickly.

The seed that doesn't get watered cannot reveal its ability to bear fruit. Collect many seeds and then, over time, look back and see which ones resonate. Sometimes we're too close to them to recognize their true potential, and other times the magical moment that inspired a seed into existence is bigger than the seed itself.

It's generally preferable to accumulate several weeks' or months' worth of ideas and then choose which of them to focus on, instead of following an urge or obligation to rush to the finish line with what is in front of us today.

The more seeds you've accumulated, the easier this is to judge. If you've collected a hundred seeds, you might find that seed number fifty-four speaks to you in a way that none of the others do. If number fifty-four is your only choice, without other seeds for context, it's more difficult to tell.

When we make assumptions about what seeds won't work or may not fit with what we believe to be our artistic identity, we may be prevented from growing as creators. Sometimes the purpose of a seed is to propel us in a completely new direction. Along the way, it may morph into something hardly resembling its original form and become our finest work yet.

At this point in time, it's helpful to think of the work as bigger than us. To cultivate a sense of awe and wonder at what's possible, and recognize that this productivity is not generated by our hand alone.

The work reveals itself as you go.

Experimentation

⊙

We have collected a handful of seeds—of starting points and potentialities. We now enter the second stage, the Experimentation phase.

Fueled by the initial hit of excitement at discovering a starting point, we play with different combinations and possibilities to see if any of them reveal how the seed wants to develop. Think of this as a search for life. We're looking to see if we can get the seeds to take root and sprout a stem.

There's no right way to experiment. Generally speaking, we want to begin interacting with the seeds, developing our starting point in different directions. We are cultivating each seed, much as a gardener creates optimal conditions to foster growth.

This is one of the fun parts of a project, because nothing is at stake. You get to play with forms and see what takes shape. There are no rules. Cultivation will look different for every artist and every seed.

If the seed is a character in a novel, perhaps we widen the world they live in, develop a backstory, or become the character and start writing from their point of view.

If the seed is a story for a film, we might want to explore various settings. It could be different countries, communities, time periods, or realities. Shakespeare's plays, for example, have been adapted into movies centered around everything from New York street gangs to samurais, from Santa Monica to outer space.

There are countless directions to explore, and we never know which will guide us to a dead end and which will lead to new realms until we test it. In the case of a song, a vocalist might respond very quickly to a musical track and the melody will immediately reveal itself. Other times, although the singer finds the musical track compelling, they will listen to it a thousand times and nothing will come from it.

In this phase, we are not looking at which iteration progresses the quickest or furthest, but which holds the most promise. We focus on the flourishing and wait to prune. We generate possibilities instead of eliminating them. Editing prematurely can close off routes that might lead to beautiful vistas previously unseen.

$$\odot$$

In the Experimentation phase, conclusions are stumbled upon. They surprise or challenge us more often than they fulfill our expectations.

Ancient Chinese alchemists searching for immortality mixed saltpeter, sulfur, and charcoal. They discovered something else: gunpowder. Countless other inventions—penicillin, plastic, pacemakers, Post-it notes—were discovered by accident. Consider how many innovations that might have changed the world have been lost because someone was so focused on their goal, they missed the revelation right in front of them.

The heart of experiment is mystery. We cannot predict where a seed will lead or if it will take root. Remain open to the new and unknown. Begin with a question mark and embark on a journey of discovery.

Take full advantage of the energy inherent in the seed itself, and do whatever's possible not to disturb it. You may be tempted to intervene and steer its development toward a specific goal or preconceived idea. This may not lead to the most productive of its possibilities at this stage of the process.

Allow the seed to follow its own path toward the sun. The

time to discriminate will come later. For now, allow space for magic to enter.

$$\odot$$

Not every seed must grow. But it may be there is a right time for each one. If a seed does not seem to be developing or responding, consider storing it rather than discarding it.

In nature, some seeds lie dormant in anticipation of the season most conducive to their growth. This is true of art as well. There are ideas whose time has not yet come. Or perhaps their time has come, but you are not yet ready to engage with them. Other times, developing a different seed may shed light on a dormant one.

Some seeds are ready to germinate instantaneously. You may start experimenting and find yourself completing the work and being pleased with the result. Or you may get halfway through the project, then feel unsure where it wants to go.

As we lose enthusiasm, we often continue to labor on a seed, believing that the work has to turn out for the better because we've invested so much time in it. If the energy continues to drop, it does not necessarily mean that the seed is bad. We just may not have found the right experiment for it. Perhaps we need to step away for a time and shift perspective. We may choose to start over with it, or set it aside for a while and sift through the others.

The outcome is not up to us. Give some attention to each seed, regardless of what you believe its potential may be, and look for a beautiful response.

If you have just one seed—a very specific vision you want to carry out—that's fine. There is no right way. You might consider the possibility, however, that it could end up being a limitation, because you are no longer taking advantage of all that you have in you. Being open to possibility gets you to a place you want to go that you may not know you wanted to get to.

If you know what you want to do and you do it, that's the work of a craftsman. If you begin with a question and use it to guide an adventure of discovery, that's the work of the artist. The surprises along the way can expand your work, and even the art form itself.

⊙

When a plant is flourishing, we can see the life spring forth from every stalk, leaf, and flower. How do we know when an idea is flourishing?

Often the most accurate signposts are emotional, not intellectual. Excitement tends to be the best barometer for selecting which seeds to focus on. When something interesting starts to come together, it arouses delight. It's an energizing feeling of wanting more. A feeling of leaning forward. Follow that energy.

During the Experimentation phase, we are paying attention to this natural reaction of enthrallment in the body. There is a time for the head work of analysis, but not yet. Here, we follow the heart. At some point, we may be able to look back and understand why the feeling arose. Other times we will not, and that's fine too. For now, this is of no concern.

⊙

If two ideas feel somewhat equal in weight, and one has clear potential to turn into something beautiful and the other shows less potential but seems more interesting, feel free to follow your interest. Base decisions on the internal feeling of being moved and notice what holds your interest. This will always be in the greatest service of the work.

Failure
is the information you need
to get where you're going.

Try Everything

Mixing blue and yellow makes green. Adding two plus two makes four.

When combining basic elements in the ordinary course of life, much is predictable.

In creating art, the sum total of the parts often defies expectation. Theory and practice don't always line up. The formula that worked yesterday might not work tomorrow. The proven solutions are sometimes the least helpful.

There is a gap between imagination and reality. An idea might seem brilliant in our mind. But once employed, it might not work at all. Another might seem dreary at first. Then, upon execution, it might be exactly what's called for.

To dismiss an idea because it doesn't work in your mind is to do a disservice to the art. The only way to truly know if any idea works is to test it. And if you're looking for the best idea, test everything.

Ask yourself as many "what if" questions as you can. What if this were the first painting anyone saw in their life? What if I removed every adverb? What if I made all the loud parts quiet? Look for different polarities and see how they affect the piece.

Perhaps take on the temporary rule that there are no bad ideas. Test them all, even the ones that seem underwhelming or unlikely to work.

This method becomes especially useful in group efforts. Often when working with others, different ideas are put forward and end up in competition. Based on experience, we may believe we can see what each person is imagining and what the result will be.

It's impossible, though, to know exactly what someone else is thinking. And if we can't predict how our own ideas will work—and we can't!—how can we draw conclusions about what someone else imagines?

Instead of talking through different solutions to work out which is best, take it out of the realm of the verbal. To truly weigh choices, it's necessary to bring them into the physical world. Have them acted out, played out, or built into a model. Descriptions do not do ideas justice.

We want to set up an environment where the decision

making occurs free of the misguiding force of persuasion. Persuasion leads to mediocrity. To be evaluated, ideas have to be seen, heard, tasted, or touched.

It's best if the person who has the idea either demonstrates it or supervises the execution until it matches what they are suggesting. This will help avoid misunderstandings.

Once the idea is witnessed in its full expression, it may turn out far better than you imagined. It may even be a perfect fit. Or it could be exactly what you expected. Something will be gained through the process, whatever the result. Give yourself permission to be wrong and experience the joy of being surprised.

When working through ways of solving a puzzle, there are no mistakes. Each unsuccessful solution gets you closer to one that works. Avoid becoming attached to the particulars of the problem. Widen your field of view. If the idea takes the project somewhere with a stronger energetic charge, follow the new direction. Demanding to control a work of art would be just as foolish as demanding that an oak tree grow according to your will.

Allow the work to grow in the direction it seeks, evolve in accordance with its natural state, and have its own life. Enjoy the journey of cycling through all permutations to reveal a work's true form.

Taking a wrong turn
allows you to see landscapes
you wouldn't otherwise have seen.

Crafting

Once a seed's code has been cracked, and its true form deciphered, the process shifts. We are no longer in the unbounded mode of discovery. A clear sense of direction has arisen.

Often unbeknownst to us, we find ourselves in the Craft phase. Now comes the labor of building.

We work to add to a foundation that has revealed itself through our experimentation. The lines have been drawn. Now we're filling in the colors.

Where the earlier phases were more free and open-ended, the inspirations and ideas that appear now are more directly related to issues at hand. We are looking for a shape that fits a specific hole, whereas before we were just looking for shapes.

In some ways, the Craft phase is one of the least glamorous parts of the artist's job. There is creativity involved, but it often carries less of the magic of exploration and more of the labor of brick-laying.

This is the point in the journey where some struggle to carry on. For now, we need to look away from the open field and turn toward a winding staircase a hundred stories tall. A long, precarious climb lies ahead.

We may be tempted to turn back and chase the thrill of feeling the light bulb flicker on above our heads. But the first two phases have little purpose or meaning on their own. Art may only exist, and the artist may only evolve, by completing the work.

$$\odot$$

How do we decide which experiment to craft?

We continue to follow hints of excitement. Each one of us has to find our own path. If several directions seem captivating, consider crafting more than one experiment at a time. Working on several often brings about a healthy sense of detachment.

When solely focused on one, it's easy to get tunnel vision. While it may appear a project's moving in the right direction, we are too closely entwined with it to truly know.

Stepping away and returning with fresh eyes brings clearer insight into next steps. Switching to other projects will engage different muscles and patterns of thinking. These may shed light on paths otherwise unseen. And this may happen over the course of days, weeks, months, or years.

Even in a single work session, moving between multiple projects can be helpful.

There are also times when a single seed has so much power that you choose to focus on it exclusively, and that is your choice to make.

In the Experimentation phase, we planted the seed, watered it, and gave the resulting plant time to grow in the sun. We let nature take its course. Now, in this third phase, we are bringing ourselves to the project to see what we can offer.

This is one reason the boundary between the Experimentation and the Craft phases isn't a linear progression. We often move back and forth between the two, because sometimes what we add isn't as good as what nature is bringing. When we realize this, we stop and go back to where nature left off.

Whereas the Experimentation phase is about what the seed has to offer, now we are applying our filter. Reviewing the totality of our experience in the world and searching for connections: What does this remind us of, what can we measure it against, what does it relate to that we've noticed over the course of our lives?

In this phase, we begin with a project that has naturally

developed. We recognize potential in it. And we see what we can add, take away, or combine to further develop it.

The Craft phase is not just a building up. It is also a breaking down. The goal of developing the work can be accomplished through a pruning process of small cuts. We decide which details and directions might be removed, so that more energy and focus can be used to feed the core elements.

$$\odot$$

While the Craft phase can be difficult, that is not always the case. There are some artists whose focus is more on formalizing an idea than executing it. And in the case of some projects, outsourcing the Craft phase is what's called for.

Many of Andy Warhol's paintings were done by other artists and by machines, while he supplied the ideas and retained authorship. Some famous California rock bands of the '60s didn't play on their own albums. And some prolific authors just invent characters and story lines, and leave it to other writers to fill out the prose.

When it comes to performing these labor-intensive aspects of the process yourself, it is not a question of right or wrong. It's project dependent. Remain open to doing whatever it takes to make the art as good as it can be, whether this means inserting yourself more into the details of the process or stepping further back from them.

For some projects, an artist may feel it's necessary to be

involved in all of the work. The physical act of crafting may give them a greater understanding of the art and more direct control over the details. Other projects may be better served if the artist acts as a maestro or designer in this phase, conducting the work of others.

Crafting can be daunting. It's helpful to think of it as another opportunity for play. For some artists, crafting is their favorite part of the process. There is a natural joy and sense of accomplishment in following a set of instructions to create something physical and beautiful. The love and care they put into this phase can be clearly recognized in the final work.

Momentum

When treated like the earlier phases, with no boundaries or time constraints, the Craft phase may extend longer than necessary.

Once enough data is collected, and the vision is clear, it can be helpful to set deadlines for completion. The options are no longer unlimited; the process is less open-ended. There may not be a clear finish line in sight, but the core elements are there.

Imagine you have a script that has been translated to storyboard. Going from storyboard to finished film is somewhat of a mechanical process. There is art and inspiration involved, and there are a million choices to be made, but the path ahead is clear. Our creative task now has narrower parameters.

If we're pleased with the blueprint, it could be constructed many different ways. As long as we continue referring back to make sure the developed project is as good as the original plan, there could be several different versions that all ring true. The power is held in the underlying structure.

If the project were a building, we're picking which materials to clad it in and what type of windows to install. You may have a preference, but the building will maintain its integrity. The details matter, but they aren't likely to sink the enterprise.

In the Craft phase, deadlines are suggested completion dates rather than set in stone. There is still an element of surprise and exploration throughout our execution, and it's possible to find ourselves at any moment back in the Experimentation phase.

While crafting, an artist might succumb to outside pressure to set a fixed release date for their project. Preparations are made. Outsiders are notified. Then sometimes, as we work diligently toward the final stage, an entirely new and preferable direction might appear. But the artist is left without the time to pursue it. And this leads to a compromised result.

The artist's goal is not merely to produce, but to make the finest work they are capable of. The business thinks in terms of quarterly earnings and production schedules. The artist thinks in terms of timeless excellence. While crafting, make deadlines for your own motivation, not necessarily to be shared with others unless it helps with accountability.

Once the Craft phase is nearing an end, then we might start thinking in terms of fixed deadlines.

⊙

Crafting contains a paradox. To create our best work, we are patient and avoid rushing the process, while at the same time we work quickly without delay.

By remaining too long in this phase, many pitfalls may arise. One is disconnection. If an artist is creating a beautiful work, and keeps endlessly crafting it beyond the need, sometimes they suddenly want to start all over. This can be because they have changed or the times have changed.

Art is a reflection of the artist's inner and outer world during the period of creation. Extending the period complicates the artist's ability to capture a state of being. The result can be a loss of connection and enthusiasm for the work over time.

Another challenge we might call *demo-itis*. Demo-itis happens when the artist has clung too tightly, for too long, to their first draft.

The danger of living with the unfinished project for too long is that the more often an artist is exposed to a particular draft of a work, the more final that form can become in their mind. A musician might record a demo of a song very quickly.

They could listen to it thousands of times and imagine developing it to all it can be. Yet when it comes time to actually make the best version of the song, the demo may be so ingrained in their head that any changes to it seem blasphemous. When we become overly attached to a premature version of the work, we do a disservice to the project's potential.

To avoid demo-itis, there is a simple technique. Unless actively working to make something better, avoid listening to it, reading it, playing it, looking at it, or showing it to friends. Work as far forward as you can while crafting and then step away, without repetitively consuming the unfinished work. By not accepting the work-in-progress as the standard version, we leave room for growth, change, and development to continue.

Keep in mind that it's also possible for something great to be made very quickly. An artist might spend five minutes sketching an idea for a project, and think very little of it. They might sense the seed of something great, and then spend hours or years trying to develop it into something more. But it is possible that the initial sketch or demo, born in all of five minutes, was actually the best version, the seed's purest expression. We may not realize this until after embellishing it or stepping away from it for a while.

Another impediment some come across is that their vision for the work exceeds their ability to manifest it. They can hear the drumline, but the rhythm is more complex than their ability to play. They can picture the dance, but their body can't perform the moves gracefully enough. It might seem as though the next step is an impossible leap.

In these moments, it's easy to feel discouraged. We mistake the fantasy version of the work in our minds for what the actual work has the possibility to become. There may indeed be times when our mental conception of a piece translates almost directly into the physical realm. At other times, it's an unrealistic idealized version. And sometimes, our vision for the work is a goal to work toward, and in the process we come to learn we'll reach a new and unexpected destination.

Falling short of grander visions might actually put the work exactly where it wants to be. Do not let the scale of your imagination get in the way of executing a more practical version of your project. We may come to realize that this version is better than the initial, seemingly impossible vision.

⊙

When you're on a roll in the Craft phase, work toward a full first draft. Maintain the momentum. If you reach a section of the work that gives you trouble, instead of letting this blockage stop you, work around it. Although your instinct may be to create sequentially, bypass the section where you're stuck, complete the other parts, then come back to it.

Sometimes solutions to these difficult pieces will reveal

themselves once the overall context has emerged. A bridge is easier to build when it's clear what's on either side of it.

Another benefit is that if you are stuck at a section in the middle, it may feel overwhelming to know you're only halfway through the work. If you finish the rest of the draft and return to the portion you skipped, it feels more easily achievable when there's only 5 or 10 percent of a project left to complete. With the end in sight, it's easier to feel motivated to finish.

If you're holding a center puzzle piece in your hand and staring at an empty tabletop, it's difficult to determine where to place it. If all of the puzzle is complete except for that one piece, then you know exactly where it goes. The same is generally true of art. The more of the work you can see, the easier it becomes to gracefully place the final details clearly where they belong.

Art is choosing to do something skillfully,
caring about the details,
bringing all of yourself
to make the finest work you can.
It is beyond ego, vanity, self-glorification,
and need for approval.

Point of View

(·)

The goal of art isn't to attain perfection. The goal is to share who we are. And how we see the world.

Artists allow us to see what we are unable to see, but somehow already know. It may be a view of the world singularly different from our own. Or one so close, it seems miraculous, as if the artist is looking through our own eyes. In either case, the artist's perception reminds us of who we are and who we can be.

One reason art resonates is because human beings are so similar. We're attracted to the shared experience held within the work. Including the imperfection in it. We recognize some part of ourselves and feel understood. And connected.

Carl Rogers said, "The personal is the universal." The personal is what makes art matter. Our point of view, not our drawing skills or musical virtuosity or ability to tell a story.

Consider the difference between art and most other trades. In the arts, our filter is the defining factor of the work. In science or technology, the aims are different. The reason we create art isn't with the intention of making something useful for someone else. We create to express who we are. Who we are and where we are on our journey.

Our point of view doesn't have to be coherent. And it's rarely simple. We may have different, and sometimes contradictory, points of view across a variety of topics. Aiming to narrow it all down to one elegant expression is unrealistic and limiting.

Whatever our perspective, so long as we share it, unaltered and undoctored, we succeed in art's fundamental purpose.

When making art, we create a mirror in which someone may see their own hidden reflection.

⊙

A point of view is different from having a point.

A point is an idea intentionally expressed. A point of view is the perspective—conscious and unconscious—through which the work emerges.

What causes us to notice a piece of art is rarely the point being made. We are drawn to the way an artist's filter refracts ideas, not to the ideas themselves.

It's of no use to know your point of view. It's already there, working in the background, ever evolving. Efforts to portray point of view on purpose often lead to a false representation. We hold on to stories about our perspective that are inaccurate and limiting.

Wayne Dyer said that when you squeeze an orange, what comes out is orange juice. When you get squeezed, whatever comes out is what's inside you. And part of that extract is the point of view you don't even know you have. It's baked into the art you make and the opinions you share.

Long after a work is completed, we may look back and understand our true point of view in it.

We don't need to make a point of making a point. It will appear when it appears. The true point is already made in the innocent act of perception and creation. Knowing this is liberating. It lifts some of the pressure. We can worry less about understanding why it works, or if others will understand where we are coming from. We are free to be present and allow the material to come through us, and free to stay out of its way when it does come through.

Much of art's greatness is felt on a gut level. Your self-expression allows the audience to have their own self-expression. If your work speaks to them, it is of no consequence if you are heard and understood.

Set aside such concerns about whether your work will be comprehended. These thoughts can only cause interference, for both the art and audience. Most people aren't interested in being told what to think or feel.

Great art is created through freedom of self-expression and received with freedom of individual interpretation.

Great art opens a conversation rather than closing it. And often this conversation is started by accident.

⊙

Most human beings like to fit in.

We adapt not only to the evolving flow of material coming through us, but the boundaries and templates of the culture around us.

Can great art come from conformity? And what is the purpose of being an artist if we deny our unique personal point of view?

Those of us choosing to live as artists embrace our filter as a gift. To reject it would be tragic. The refracted light it projects is our own singular landscape of artistic possibility. How can a piece of art ever truly be a guilty pleasure?

⊙

The Beatles were inspired by American rock and roll, artists like Chuck Berry and the Shirelles. But when they played, it was different. It wasn't different because they wanted it to be so. It was different because they were different. And the world responded.

There are countless examples of imitation turning into legitimate innovation. Having a romanticized vision of an artist, genre, or tradition may allow you to create something new, because you see it from a different perspective than those closer to it. Sergio Leone's Spaghetti Westerns are abstract psychedelic mythology compared with the American Westerns of the 1940s and '50s that he hoped to mirror.

It's impossible to imitate another artist's point of view. We can only swim in the same waters. So feel free to copy the works that inspire you on the road to finding your own voice. It's a time-tested tradition.

⊙

In the culture, there's always a dialogue between the past, the present, and the future, even when it's not clear what the influence is. As creators and enthusiasts, we share and receive points of view in order to participate in and further this exchange.

When we hear something new, it provides insight into where we've been and where else we could go. We may have thought we could only move forward. But when someone turns left, it shows we can also go right. And then our right turn may perhaps inspire someone else to explore an entirely new direction.

It's a symbiotic loop. The culture informs who you are. And who you are informs your work. Your work then feeds back into the culture.

This constant march into the unknown would not exist without the simultaneous sharing of millions of divergent points of view.

Expressing oneself in the world and creativity are the same. It may not be possible to know who you are without somehow expressing it.

Breaking the Sameness

○

There are times during the Craft phase when you hit a wall and the work isn't getting any better. Before stepping away from the piece, it's worth finding a way to break the sameness and refresh your excitement in the work, as if engaging with it for the first time.

In the recording studio, I occasionally suggest exercises to artists with this goal in mind. We attempt them without expectations regarding outcome. The intention is simply to rekindle excitement and access new ways of performance.

Several of these exercises follow. Whether or not you find yourself at an impasse, perhaps they can inspire similar experiments in your chosen field.

Small Steps

To create movement for a musician who was blocked, we offered him a small task: write just one line every day. It didn't matter how good or bad he felt about the line, as long as he committed to writing it. If more came through, that was fine but not necessary. By breaking down what seemed insurmountable into single lines, he was able to reopen the creative channel and eventually began composing entire songs again. This happened much more quickly than expected.

Change the Environment

If we're looking for a performance of a different nature, it can help to change an element of the environment. Turning off the lights and playing in the dark can create a shift in consciousness and break the chain of sameness from performance to performance. Other shifts we've experimented with include having a singer hold the microphone instead of standing in front of it, and recording early in the morning instead of at night. To access a greater degree of variation, one vocalist chose to hang upside down while singing.

Change the Stakes

Besides changing the external environment, you can also change the inner. If a band imagines that this is the last time they'll ever play a particular song, they're likely to perform it differently than if it's just another take. Other times lower stakes, such as doing a rehearsal prior to recording, may bring out the best performance.

Invite an Audience

When an artist thrives on being in front of a crowd, we may bring in several people to watch a session. Being observed changes how an artist acts. Even if the audience consists only of one person who isn't part of the project, that can be enough. While some artists may overdo a performance for an audience and others may hold back, most tend to be more focused with someone else present. Even if your art is non-performative, such as writing or cooking, it will still likely change with an observer present. The goal is to find the specific parameters in each case that bring out your best.

Change the Context

There are times when a singer doesn't connect with a song, like an actor whose line reading falls flat. It can be helpful to create a new meaning or an additional backstory to a song's lyrics. A love song might sound different if sung to a long-lost soulmate, a partner of thirty years that you don't get along with, a person you saw on the street but never spoke to, or your mother.

With one artist, I suggested singing a love song written to a woman as a devotional to God instead. We can try many different permutations while singing the same song, without changing any of the lyrics, to see which version brings out the best performance.

Alter the Perspective

A technique we sometimes use in the studio is to turn up the volume on the headphones extremely loud. When every sound explodes in your ears, there's a natural tendency to play much quieter to restore the balance. It's a forced perspective change, and can bring out a very delicate performance. Even vocals will be whispered, because anything more than that would be overwhelming. Conversely, to coax someone to sing louder, with more energy, I might ask them to turn the vocal volume down in their headphones so their voice is drowned out by the music. Whatever the situation, if a task is challenging to accomplish, there's often a way to design the surroundings to naturally encourage the performance you're striving for.

In a concert, setting up the lighting so that the performer either sees the crowd and the faces in it or can't see anyone at all will alter the performance. If a performer uses in-ear monitors and all they hear is the music they're playing and not the audience response, it will be very different than if the screaming of the crowd is mixed in. It's worth experimenting with different scenarios to observe what they bring out and to find the performance you want.

Write for Someone Else

In the case of a musician who typically writes their own material, I'll suggest, "Imagine that a favorite artist asked you to write a song for their next album. What would that song sound like?"

By creating something you'd be excited to hear your favorite artist perform, it depersonalizes the process and can allow the writer to break free of themselves. A quintessential song of female empowerment, "(You Make Me Feel Like) A Natural Woman" was written by Carole King and Gerry Goffin. King—and then, of course, Aretha Franklin—sang it. I was surprised to learn that Goffin wrote the lyrics and King the music.

At times, I will ask the musician to select an artist whose lyrics and point of view are very different from their own, as a way to avoid the sameness that can occur in a career over time. If an artist is normally full of braggadocio, we may choose a more vulnerable, soft-spoken lyricist. If you tend to write in style x, it can be interesting to choose an artist who is the polar opposite of x. This doesn't mean the song will be good. It's just interesting to see where it leads. And sometimes it leads you right where you're going.

Like the other exercises, this can be applied to any craft.

If you're a painter, creating an original new work by your favorite artist can open a channel and lead to interesting results. Many artists have a perceived idea of what's in their wheelhouse, and that's ultimately a limitation. So it's helpful to step out of yourself and into someone else's wheelhouse.

Add Imagery

I was working on an album and the band was struggling with the keyboard solo. The mood wasn't right. We wanted something more grand. So instead of a musical reference, we created a scene. We came up with a description of the aftermath of a battle: "Imagine there's a beautiful green hill covered in trees and flora, just breathtaking, and a battle has just ended. Smoke drifts off the hill and reveals wounded soldiers scattered along it, waiting for help to arrive." We painted the scene very vividly, then said, "Play the solo like that," and hit *record*. The keyboardist began playing beautifully.

Since then, it's been a technique we've continued to use. Often, we don't even know what the connections are between the image and what we want to hear. Thinking of a specific image or story, or imagining that you're scoring a film and then starting to play, will often bring a stronger direction to a meandering tune.

Limit the Information

When a songwriter sends a demo of a track for a band to record in the studio, I don't want the musicians to in any way be informed by the musical choices made for the demo. So I'll typically have one musician, usually a guitar player, listen to it and learn the chords, notate them on the lyric sheet, and give that to the band.

The guitar player and the singer may then perform it, with no suggestion of rhythm other than the speed implied by the way they play it.

When you're working with great musicians, this leaves them free to bring in more of themselves. Rather than recording a good version of the demo, they will use the full range of their creativity and decision-making abilities to take the song somewhere new and often unexpected. If the results aren't great after trying different approaches, they can always listen to the demo at that point, though that rarely happens.

The general principle is to be protective and limit people you're working with from experiencing things that could interfere with their creative process. Limit the information to the barest of sketches. If you want creators to bring all of themselves to something, give them the most freedom to create. If you give a screenwriter a book, an outline, or a sentence to turn into a script, each will lead to a very different screenplay.

These exercises are not set in stone. The intention is to establish different perspectives or conditions, and see where you or your collaborators end up. Consider creating your own versions of these experiments. Or if using these specific ones, feel free to change the parameters as you're working or remove them altogether when the time is right. The actual exercises are of little importance. The purpose is to set up a structure to go beyond your usual method and find new ways forward.

Completion

As the work improves through the Craft phase, you'll come to the point where all of the options available to you have been explored sufficiently.

The seed has achieved its full expression and you've pruned it to your satisfaction. Nothing is left to add or take away. The work's essence rings clear. There's a sense of fulfillment in these moments.

From here, we advance into the final movement of the creative process.

In the Completion phase, we leave behind discovery and building. With a beautiful volume of material crafted before us, the final form is refined to be released into the world.

The finishing touches and fine-tuning are different for every project. They may be as simple as putting a frame on a painting, color correcting a film, tweaking a song's final mix, or rereading a manuscript to make sure the phrasing is just right.

As with the other stages of the creative act, the Completion phase isn't a clear line you cross in a forward journey. In the process of preparing your work to share, you may realize there's more to be done. A revision, an addition, a deletion, or some other change may be called for. So you step back to Craft or Experiment, and work your way forward once more.

We can think of the Completion phase as the last stop on an assembly line. The finished piece is examined to ensure it meets your highest standards. If it doesn't meet them, you send it back to be improved. Once it does, you sign off on it, let it go, and begin the next chapter of your life's work—whatever that may be.

$$\odot$$

Once you feel a project is close to completion, it can be helpful to open the work to other perspectives.

The primary aim is not to receive notes or opinions. This is your work, your expression. You are the only audience that matters. The intention is for you to experience the work anew.

When playing music for someone else, we hear it differently than when we listen to it ourselves. It's as if borrowing a second set of ears. We're not necessarily looking for an outside perspective. We are more interested in widening our own.

If we write an essay and give it to a friend, before even hearing their perspective, our relationship to the work changes. Give it to a mentor and our perspective shifts in a different way. We interrogate ourselves when we offer our work up to others. We ask the questions we didn't ask ourselves when we were making it. Sharing it in this limited capacity brings our underlying doubts to light.

If someone chooses to share feedback, listen to understand the person, not the work. People will tell you more about themselves than about the art when giving feedback. We each see a unique world.

Occasionally, a comment will strike home. It will resonate with something we feel, either in our awareness or just behind it, and we may discover room for improvement. Other times, a judgment will hit a nerve, and we find ourselves defending the work or losing faith.

In these moments, it may be helpful to step away, reset, and return with a neutral mind. Criticism allows us to engage with our work in a new way. We may agree or we may double down on our original instincts.

Sometimes a challenge allows us to focus on an aspect of the work and realize it's more important than we previously thought. In the process, we access deeper wells of understanding into the work and ourselves.

As you collect feedback, the solutions offered may not always seem helpful. Before discarding them, take a moment to see if they're pointing to an underlying problem you hadn't noticed.

For example, if there's a suggestion to remove the bridge of a song, you might interpret that as "it's worth reexamining the bridge." And then set about looking at it in the context of the entire piece.

If you've truly created an innovative work, it's likely to alienate as many people as it attracts. The best art divides the audience. If everyone likes it, you probably haven't gone far enough.

In the end, you are the only one who has to love it. This work is for you.

$$\odot$$

When is the work done?

There is no formula or method for finding this answer. It is an intuition:

The work is done when you feel it is.

Although we avoid deadlines early in the process, in the Completion phase, a due date could help bring time into focus and support you in completing the work.

Art doesn't get made on the clock. But it can get finished on the clock.

Some find this phase to be the most difficult part of the process. They resist letting go with a stubborn ferocity. Up until this point, the clay is still soft. Everything can change. Once fixed, we lose control. This fear of permanence is common beyond art. It is known as commitment phobia.

When the last chapter is about to end, we may create excuses to put off the completion of the work.

It can be a sudden loss of faith in the project. Deciding it's no longer good enough. We find flaws that don't really exist. We make inconsequential changes. We sense the distant mirage of some better creative option that hasn't been discovered yet. And if only we just keep working, it might arrive someday.

When you believe the work before you is the single piece that will forever define you, it's difficult to let it go. The urge for perfection is overwhelming. It's too much. We are frozen, and sometimes end up convincing ourselves that discarding the entire work is the only way to move forward.

The only art the world gets to enjoy is from creators who've overcome these hurdles and released their work. Perhaps still greater artists existed than the ones we know, but they were never able to make this leap.

Releasing a work into the world becomes easier when we remember that each piece can never be a total reflection of us, only a reflection of who we are in this moment. If we wait, it's no longer today's reflection. In a year, we may be guided to create a piece that looks nothing like it. There is a timeliness to the work. The passing of seasons could dissipate the value the work holds for us.

Hanging on to your work is like spending years writing the same entry in a diary. Moments and opportunities are lost. The next works are robbed of being brought to life.

How many pages will be left empty because your process was dampened by doubt and deliberation? Keep this question in the front of your mind. It might allow you to move forward more freely.

In an environment where nothing is permanent, we produce static artifacts. Mementos of spirit. We hope they'll live forever, holding resonance through each passing decade. Some might, many won't. It's impossible to know. We can only keep building.

When you and the work are in sync, there's a time to put it out and move on.

Each new project is another opportunity to communicate what's coming through you. It's another chance at bat. Another opportunity to connect. Another page filled in the diary of your inner life.

⊙

Concerns about releasing a work into the world may be rooted in deeper anxieties. It could be a fear of being judged, misunderstood, ignored, or disliked. Will more ideas come? Will they ever be this good again?

Will anyone even care?

Part of the process of letting go is releasing any thoughts of how you or your piece will be received. When making art, the audience comes last. Let's not consider how a piece will be received or our release strategy until the work is finished and we love it.

This is different from a work being perfect. We can engage with any of the works we've been a part of and recognize things wrong with them. Maybe we didn't in the moment we finished them, but when looking back we often do. There are forever changes to be made. There is no right version. Every work of art is simply an iteration.

One of the greatest rewards of making art is our ability to share it. Even if there is no audience to receive it, we build the muscle of making something and putting it out into the world. Finishing our work is a good habit to develop. It boosts confidence. Despite our insecurities, the more times we can bring ourselves to release our work, the less weight insecurity has.

Avoid overthinking. When you're happy with the work and you're moved to share it with a friend, it might be time to share it with the world as well.

This final phase is a fertile time to plant a new crop of seeds. The excitement of what's coming next can generate the vital energy needed to bring the current work to its close.

You may find it a struggle to keep yourself focused on the project at hand when new ideas start coming at you. This is a good problem to have. Riding the life force of the project to come often breaks us out of the trance of the present piece. We can't wait to finish, because there's another idea calling that lights us up.

Is it time for the next project
because the clock or calendar
says it's time,
or because the work itself
says it's time?

The Abundant Mindset

A river of material flows through us. When we share our works and our ideas, they are replenished. If we block the flow by holding them all inside, the river cannot run and new ideas are slow to appear.

In the abundant mindset, the river never runs dry. Ideas are always coming through. And an artist is free to release them with the faith that more will arrive.

If we live in a mindset of scarcity, we hoard great ideas. A comedian may be presented with a perfect opportunity to tell a favorite new joke they've written, but instead will hold it back waiting for a more high-profile occasion. When we use our material, new content comes through. And the more we share, the more our skills improve.

Choosing to live in scarcity leads to stagnation. If we work on one project forever, we never get to make another. The fear of drought and the impulse for perfectionism prevent us from moving on and block the river's flow.

Each mindset evokes a universal rule: whatever we concentrate on, we get.

If the mind creates a world that is limited, where we think we don't have enough worthwhile ideas or material, we will not see the inspiration the universe is providing.

And the river slows.

In the abundant world, we have a greater capacity to complete and release our work. When there are so many ideas available and so much great art to make, we are compelled to engage, let go, and move forward.

If there is only one work to do, and we intend to retire when it's done, there is no impetus to finish. If each piece is approached as our life's defining work, we revise and overwrite endlessly, aiming for the unrealistic ideal of perfection.

A musician may delay releasing an album for fear they haven't taken the songs as far as they can go. Yet an album is only a diary entry of a moment of time, a snapshot reflection of who the artist is for that period. And no one diary entry is our life story.

Our life's work is far greater than any individual container. The works we do are at most chapters. There will always be a new chapter, and another after that. Though some might be better than others, that is not our concern. Our objective is to be free to close one chapter and move on to the next, and to continue that process for as long as it pleases us.

Your old work isn't better than your new work. And your new work isn't better than the old. There will be highs and lows throughout an artist's life. To assume there was a golden period and you're past it is only true if you accept that premise. Putting your best effort in at each moment, in each chapter, is all we can ever hope to accomplish.

There is always more we can improve or another version to be made. We could work on something for another two years, and it will be different. But there's no way to know if it will be better or worse—only different. Just as you will be. And you may have evolved past the work you spent years laboring on. The direct reflection of you has faded. The work begins to look like an old photo instead of a mirror image. It's dispiriting to complete and share a work you've lost connection with.

The recognition of abundance fills us with hope that our brightest ideas still await us and our greatest work is yet to come. We are able to live in an energized state of creative momentum, free to make things, let them go, make the next thing, and let it go. With each chapter we make, we gain experience, improve at our craft, and inch closer to who we are.

The Experimenter and the Finisher

In their nature, many artists lean toward one of two categories: Experimenters or Finishers.

Experimenters are partial to dreaming and play, finding it more difficult to complete and release their work.

Finishers are the mirror image, a backward reflection. They move quickly to the end point with immediate clarity. They are less interested in exploring the possibilities and alternatives that the Experimentation and Craft phases can suggest.

Each might find it helpful to borrow from the other.

Finishers might benefit from taking more time in the early phases. Writing beyond the minimum requirement, experimenting with other materials, considerations, and perspectives. Allowing themselves space for improvisation and surprise in the process.

Experimenters might benefit from taking an aspect of the work through to completion. It might be a drawing, a song, or the chapter of a book. Even making one foundational decision from which to build can help.

Take the example of an album. If you're a musician struggling with ten songs, narrow your focus to two. When we make the task more manageable and focused, a change occurs. And completing even a small segment builds confidence.

Going from two to three is easier than going from zero to two. And if you happen to get stuck on three, then skip it and get four and five done.

Complete as many elements of the project as you can without getting hung up. It's much easier to circle back once the workload is reduced. Often the knowledge we gain from finishing the other pieces becomes a key to overcoming earlier obstacles.

Temporary Rules

⊙

Much of the artistic process involves ignoring rules, letting go of rules, undermining rules, and rooting out rules that we didn't know we were following. There is also a place for imposing rules. For using rules as a tool to define a given project.

When there are no material, time, and budget constraints, you have unlimited options. When you accept limitations, your range of choices is reduced. Whether imposed by design or by necessity, it's helpful to see limitations as opportunities.

Think of this as setting a palette for each project. Within these constraints, the problem-solving aspects become more specific, and the most obvious solutions may not be available. This culling can help give new work its character and set it apart from past efforts, with potential for groundbreaking results. Novel problems lead to original solutions.

Georges Perec wrote an entire book without using the most common letter of the French alphabet: *e*. It went on to become one of the most celebrated experimental works in modern literature.

The painter Yves Klein decided to limit his palette to one color. This led him to discover a shade of blue no one had ever seen before. The shade itself was seen by many as effectively becoming the art, and was later named "International Klein Blue."

The director Lars von Trier came up with ten rules, Dogme 95 The Vow of Chastity, designed to reduce the artificiality of filmmaking. They were as follows:

1. Shooting must be performed on location, without providing props or sets that don't logically exist within that setting.
2. Diegetic sound only. Sounds must never be produced, such as music that does not exist within the scene.
3. All shots must be handheld. Movement, immobility, and stability must be attained by hand.
4. The film must be in color, with no special lighting. If there's not enough exposure, a single lamp may be attached to the camera.

5. There can be no optical work or lens filters.

6. No 'superficial' action (such as staged murders, elaborate stunts, etc.).

7. Geographical alienation is strictly forbidden, meaning the film must take place here and now.

8. No genre movies.

9. Academy 35mm is the only accepted film format.

10. Directors must not be credited.

Three years after the manifest's announcement, the first official Dogme 95 film was released by Thomas Vinterberg. Titled *The Celebration (Festen),* the film was an instant critical success, winning the Jury Prize at the 1998 Cannes Film Festival.

Inspired by Von Trier, the keyboardist Money Mark made a similar set of rules, applicable to music, to record one of his most highly regarded albums.

The rules of baseball or basketball define the game and are rarely altered. Innovation exists only within those rules. As artists, we get to create a new set of rules each and every time we play. After careful consideration, we may choose to break them in the midst of a project if a discovery impels us. While it's easy to make these changes, there's little use to rules if they are not taken seriously.

There are no bad rules or good rules. Only rules that fit the situation and serve the art, or those that don't. If the goal is to create the most beautiful work possible, then whatever directives are truly in service to that end are the right ones to use.

⊙

The imposition of rules is most valuable for an artist who has already made some work. If you're established in a craft or field, temporary rules may be useful to break a pattern. They can challenge you to become better, to innovate, and to bring out a new side of yourself or your work.

Some virtuoso artists choose to switch to less familiar instruments or mediums, because the challenge reveals them as the artist they truly are, without the distraction of their technical skill.

Set parameters that force you out of your comfort zone. If you always write on a laptop, try using a yellow legal pad. If you're right-handed, paint using your left hand. If you base your melodies on instrumentals, write one acappella. If you film using professional equipment, consider making an entire movie with only the camera in your phone. If you always prepare for acting roles through research, try a blind improvisation.

Whatever you choose, decide on a framework that breaks your normal rhythm and see where it leads. Just by the nature of the limitations you set, the work will be different from what you've done before. It is of little importance whether it's better. The purpose is self-discovery.

If you typically write short paragraphs, you may decide to experiment with long paragraphs. You may not like the new form as much, but you'll probably learn something in the process that will improve the short paragraphs. By breaking the rules, you'll come to have a greater understanding of your past choices.

An issue for some successful artists when considering changes in style or method is concern for their following. They ask: *Will the audience come along for the ride?*

In exploring new horizons, you may very well lose some fans. New fans may also appear. Whatever the case, the decision to limit your work to the familiar is a disservice to both yourself and your audience. The energy of wonder and discovery can get lost when treading the same ground over and over again.

A rule is a way of structuring awareness.

Greatness

Imagine going to live on a mountaintop by yourself, forever. You build a home that no one will ever visit. Still, you invest the time and effort to shape the space in which you'll spend your days.

The wood, the plates, the pillows—all magnificent. Curated to your taste.

This is the essence of great art. We make it for no other purpose than creating our version of the beautiful, bringing all of ourself to every project, whatever its parameters and constraints. Consider it an offering, a devotional act. We do the best, as we see the best—with our own taste. No one else's.

We create our art so we may inhabit it ourselves.

Measurement of greatness is subjective, like art itself. There is no hard metric. We are performing for an audience of one.

If you think, "I don't like it but someone else will," you are not making art for yourself. You've found yourself in the business of commerce, which is fine; it just may not be art. There's no bright line between the two. The more formulaic your creation is, the more it hugs the shore of what's been popular, the less like art it's likely to be. And in fact, creativity in that spirit often fails even at its own goals. There is no more valid metric to predict what someone else might enjoy than us liking it ourselves.

Fear of criticism. Attachment to a commercial result. Competing with past work. Time and resource constraints. The aspiration of wanting to change the world. And any story beyond "I want to make the best thing I can make, whatever it is" are all undermining forces in the quest for greatness.

Instead of focusing on what making this will bring you, focus on what you contribute to this art to make it the best it could possibly be, with no limitation.

If you're creating something with a solely functional purpose, such as a car designed to reach a certain top speed, other intentions may matter. If your project is purely artistic, then redirect your inner voice to focus on pure creative intent.

With the objective of simply doing great work, a ripple effect occurs. A bar is set for everything you do, which may not only lift your work to new heights, but raise the vibration of your entire life. It may even inspire others to do their best work. Greatness begets greatness. It's infectious.

Success

How shall we measure success?

It isn't popularity, money, or critical esteem. Success occurs in the privacy of the soul. It comes in the moment you decide to release the work, before exposure to a single opinion. When you've done all you can to bring out the work's greatest potential. When you're pleased and ready to let go.

Success has nothing to do with variables outside yourself.

To move forward is an aspect of success. This happens when we finish a work, share it, and begin a new project.

Whatever comes after this quiet feeling of accomplishment is subject to market conditions. Conditions beyond us. Our calling is to make beautiful works to the best of our ability. Sometimes they will be applauded or rewarded, sometimes not. If we second-guess our inner knowing to attempt to predict what others may like, our best work will never appear.

⊙

Popular success is a poor barometer of work and worth. In order for a work to connect commercially, stars must align and none of them relate to how good the project is. It might be the timing, the distribution mechanism, the mood of the culture, or a connection to current events.

If a global catastrophe happens on the same day a project comes out, the project might be overshadowed. If you've made a stylistic change, your fans may not initially be receptive to it. If a highly anticipated work by another artist is released on the same day, your project may not land with the same impact. Most variables are completely out of our control. The only ones we can control are doing our best work, sharing it, starting the next, and not looking back.

⊙

It's not uncommon to long for outward success, hopeful it will fill a void inside ourselves. Some imagine achievement as a remedy to fix or heal a sense of not being enough.

Artists who work diligently to accomplish this are rarely prepared for the reality of it. Most aspects of popularity are not as advertised. And the artist is often just as empty as they were before, probably more so.

If you are living in the belief that success will cure your pain, when the treatment comes and doesn't work, it can lead to hopelessness. A depression can accompany the realization that what you've spent most of your life chasing hasn't fixed your insecurities and vulnerabilities. More likely, with the stakes and consequences now higher, it has only amplified the pressure. And we are never taught how to handle this epic disappointment.

A loyal audience can begin to feel like a prison. A musician might begin working in a particular genre because it's the one they love, and might achieve great success with it. If their taste changes, they may feel chained to the old way, because there are now managers, publicists, agents, assistants, and others who have a stake in their commercial success. On a personal level, they may even tie their own identity to the style of work they've inhabited in the past.

Whenever an instinct toward movement and evolution arises, it's wise to listen to it. The alternative—being trapped by a fear of losing ground—is a dead end. You may lose your enjoyment and belief in the work because it's no longer true to you. As a result, the work may ring hollow and fail to engage the audience anyway.

Consider that it might not have been your initial style

that attracted success, but your personal passion within it. So if your passion changes course, follow it. Your trust in your instincts and excitement are what resonate with others.

The same outcome can be viewed as a great success or a terrible failure, depending on the perspective. This perception can have a momentum that's carried forth through the writer's career. Being labeled a failure with a work that was successful by most other metrics can make moving forward that much more difficult to navigate.

This is why it's grounding to protect your personal understanding of success. And to make each new work, no matter where you stand on the ladder of public perception, like you have nothing to lose.

If we can tune in to the idea
of making things and sharing them
without being attached to the outcome,
the work is more likely
to arrive in its truest form.

Connected Detachment
(Possibility)

Consider detaching from the story of your life as it's happening.

The manuscript of the novel you've worked on for years is lost in a fire. Your romantic relationship breaks up when you thought it was going well. You lose a job you care about. As hard as it may seem, seek to experience events like these as if you're watching a movie. You're observing a dramatic scene where the protagonist faces a seemingly insurmountable challenge.

It's you, but it's not you.

Instead of sinking into the pain of heartbreak or the stress of being laid off or the grief of loss, if practicing detachment the response might be: *I wasn't expecting that plot twist. I wonder what's going to happen to our hero next.*

There's always a next scene, and that next scene may be one of great beauty and fulfillment. The hard times were the required setup to allow these new possibilities to come into being.

The outcome is not the outcome. The darkness is not an end point, nor is the daylight. They live in a continually unfolding, mutually dependent cycle. Neither is bad or good. They simply exist.

This practice—of never assuming an experience you have is the whole story—will support you in a life of open possibility and equanimity. When we obsessively focus on these events, they may appear catastrophic. But they're just a small aspect of a larger life, and the further you zoom back, the smaller each experience becomes.

Zoom in and obsess. Zoom out and observe. We get to choose.

When we reach an impasse, we may experience feelings of hopelessness. The ability to stay out of the story, zoom back, and see new pathways into and around a challenge will be of boundless use.

If we allow this principle to work on us as we work on it, our imagination frees us from the web of personal and cultural stories engulfing us. Art has the power to snap us out of our transfixion, open our minds to what's possible, and reconnect with the eternal energy that moves through all things.

The Ecstatic

Have you ever felt pulled in, as if entranced, while listening to a piece of music? How about while reading a book or gazing at a painting?

This may be one of the reasons you're drawn to creative work to begin with—the memory, the recurring experience, of sensory joy. It's like biting into a piece of fruit at the peak of its ripeness.

Now think of everything held in a work that comes before the moment of perfect balance. All the experiments that miss the mark. The ideas that go nowhere. The difficult decisions that are made. The tiny adjustments that seem to change everything.

What is the test an artist uses in those crucial moments during the process? How do you know when the work—and the working—is good? How can you tell when you're moving in the right direction? What does forward motion look like?

You could say it's a feeling. An inner voice. A silent whisper that makes you laugh. An energy that enters the room and possesses the body. Call it joy, awe, or elation. When a sense of harmony and fulfillment suddenly prevails.

It is an arising of the ecstatic.

The ecstatic is our compass, pointing to our true north. It arises genuinely in the process of creation. You're working and struggling, and suddenly you notice a shift. A revelation. A small tweak is made, a new angle is revealed, and it takes your breath away.

It can arise from even the most seemingly mundane detail. The change of a word in a sentence. Instantly, the passage morphs from nonsense to poetry, and everything falls into place.

An artist will be in the throes of creation, and the work may seem unremarkable for a while. Suddenly, a shift occurs or a moment is revealed, and the same piece now seems extraordinary.

So little was needed to make the leap from mediocrity to greatness. The leap can't always be understood, but when it happens, it's clear and enlivening.

This can occur at any point during a project. You may be

moving along in the neutral zone for some time. You hit a new note, and suddenly you feel magnetized. You're engaged. You lean forward and feel a rush of energy, like an answered prayer.

This feeling is the affirmation that you're on the right path. It is a nudge to keep going. A sign that you're working in the direction of greatness, that there is deeper truth in what you're doing. It's grounded in something worthy.

This epiphany is the heart of creativity. It's something we feel in our whole body. It causes us to snap to attention and quicken our heartbeat, or to laugh in surprise. It gives us a glimpse of a higher ideal, opening new possibilities in us that we didn't know were there. It is so invigorating that it makes all of the laborious, less interesting parts of the work worth doing.

We are mining for these events: the moments when the dots connect. We revel in the satisfaction of seeing the whole shape come into clear focus.

⊙

The nature of the ecstatic is animalistic. A visceral, body-centered reaction, not a cerebral one. It doesn't have to make sense. It is not meant to be understood. It is there to guide us.

The intellect may help complete the work, and it may decipher what is driving our delight in hindsight, but the making of art depends on getting out of our heads. Part of the beauty of creation is that we can surprise ourselves, and make something greater than we're capable of understanding at the time, if we ever can.

Latent ideas and emotions hiding in deeper layers of the psyche may find their way into our lyrics, scenes, and canvases. Many artists come to realize long after their work is released that it was actually a shockingly vulnerable and cryptic form of public confession. A part of themselves was trying to find resolution or to find a voice.

The depth of our work doesn't necessarily matter. Though when you follow your instinctual bodily reactions, you'll often arrive at more profound places than you otherwise would.

The ecstatic can be experienced in different ways. At times, it's a sense of relaxed excitement, like when you're asked a question that you don't think you know the answer to yet you find yourself responding perfectly from a deeper sense of knowing. A rising of energy in the body may create a calm, invigorating confidence.

Other times, it is a moment of astonishment, when you feel emotions so powerful that you can't believe they're happening. They jolt your reality and push you into a sense of disbelief. Like realizing you're driving into oncoming traffic.

Then there's a third kind, where you're gently transported out of reality, without knowing it. While listening to a song, you may find yourself closing your eyes and being taken somewhere. When it ends, you're almost bewildered to find yourself back in your body. As if awakening from a spontaneous dream.

Tune in to these feelings in your creative work. Look for the reactions within. Of all the experiences that occur during the creative process, touching the ecstatic and allowing it to guide our hand are the most profound and precious.

Point of Reference

Every so often, you hear a new recording by an artist you've been following for a period of time who's breaking strange new ground.

It feels odd to hear the work at first. It seems unfamiliar. You have no context for it. You may not be sure you like it. You may even reject it.

Still you're compelled to listen again and again. A new pattern begins to emerge in your brain. What was strange becomes a little more familiar. You start to see how it connects to what came before. It begins to click in your mind, whether you like it or not.

And then one day you realize you can't live without it.

When a beloved artist thwarts our expectations or a new artist defies known precedents, it can be confusing. Initially, the work may feel unsatisfying or of no interest whatsoever. Once we get over the hump of adapting ourselves to the new palette, these can end up being our favorite works. Conversely, works we like immediately might not have that same power down the road.

The very same phenomenon can happen while making our own work.

If you're looking for solutions to a problem, or a new project to begin, you may react in a strongly negative way to an option that springs forth. This can be when the idea is so new that you don't have any context for it. When we don't have context, new ideas appear foreign or awkward.

Sometimes the ideas that least match our expectations are the most innovative. By definition, revolutionary ideas have no context. They invent their own.

When we initially experience the radically new, our first instinct might be to push it away and think, *this isn't for me.* And sometimes it may not be. Other times it could lead to our most enduring, important work.

Be aware of strong responses. If you're immediately turned off by an experience, it's worth examining why. Powerful reactions often indicate deeper wells of meaning. And perhaps by exploring them, you'll be led to the next step on your creative path.

Non-Competition

(•)

Art is about the maker.

Its aim: to be an expression of who we are.

This makes competition absurd. Every artist's playing field is specific to them. You are creating the work that best represents you. Another artist is making the work that best represents them. The two cannot be measured against one another. Art relates to the artist making it, and the unique contribution they are bringing to the culture.

Some may argue that competition inspires greatness. The challenge of exceeding what others have accomplished can act as an incentive to push our creative limits. In most cases, though, this energy of competition oscillates at a lower vibration.

Wanting to outperform another artist or make a work better than theirs rarely results in true greatness. Nor is it a mindset that has a healthy impact on the rest of our lives. As Theodore Roosevelt pointed out, comparison is the thief of joy. Besides, why would we want to create with the purpose of diminishing someone else?

When another great work inspires us to elevate our own, however, the energy is different. Seeing the bar raised in our field can encourage us to reach even higher. This energy of rising-to-meet is quite different from that of conquering.

When Brian Wilson first heard the Beatles' *Rubber Soul*, his mind was blown. "If I ever do anything in my life, I'm going to make that good an album," he thought at the time. He went on to explain, "I was so happy to hear it that I went and started writing 'God Only Knows.'"

Being made happy by someone else's best work, and then letting it inspire you to rise to the occasion, is not competition. It's collaboration.

When Paul McCartney heard the resulting Beach Boys album, *Pet Sounds*, he too was blown away and reduced to tears, proclaiming "God Only Knows" was to his ears the best song ever written. Buoyed by the experience, the Beatles played *Pet Sounds* over and over while creating another masterpiece, *Sgt. Pepper's Lonely Hearts Club Band.* "Without *Pet Sounds, Sgt. Pepper* never would have happened," Beatles producer George Martin said. *"Pepper* was an attempt to equal *Pet Sounds."*

This creative back-and-forth wasn't based on commercial competition, it was based on mutual love. And we are all the beneficiaries of this upward spiral toward magnificence.

No system exists that can rank which work is most reflective of the maker. Great art is an invitation, calling to creators everywhere to strive for still higher and deeper levels.

⊙

There is another type of competitiveness that might be seen as an infinite gain: a story that can continue to unfold over the course of an artist's life. This is the competition with the self.

Think of self-competition as a quest for evolution. The object is not to beat our other work. It's to move things forward and create a sense of progression. Growth over superiority.

Our ability and taste may evolve, yielding different works over time, but none can be evaluated as more or less than another. They are different snapshots of who we are, and who we were. They are all our best work in the moment they were created.

With each new project, we are challenging ourselves to most beautifully reflect what's living in us at that particular window of time.

In this spirit of self-competition, task yourself to go further and push into the unexpected. Don't stop even at greatness. Venture beyond.

Essence

(•)

All the work we do, no matter how intricate, holds an under-lying essence. A core identity or fundamental structure, like a skeleton supporting flesh. Some might call it an "is-ness."

If a child draws a picture of a house, it may have a window, a roof, and a door. If you take away the window and look at the picture, it's still a house. If you take away the door, it's still a house. If you take away the roof and the outer walls, and leave the window and the door, it is no longer clear whether it's still a house.

In the same way, each piece of art has a unique, life-giving feature that makes it what it is. It might be the theme, the organizing principle, the artist's point of view, the quality of the performance, the materials, the mood conveyed, or a combination of elements. Any of these can play a role in forming the essence.

If a sculptor makes a work out of stone or out of clay, the experience of that work is very different. Yet a work of stone and one of clay can have the same essence.

The essence is always there, and our job in the Craft phase is not to obscure it. A work's essence may also change, from the time you start until the time you finish. As you refine the work, add elements, and move pieces around, a new, different essence may emerge.

Sometimes you may not yet know the essence when you're engaged in the work. You're merely experimenting and playing. When you end up with something you like, you may come to realize what the essence is.

Distilling a work to get it as close to its essence as possible is a useful and informative practice. Notice how many pieces you can remove before the work you're making ceases to be the work you're making.

Refine it to the point where it is stripped bare, in its least decorative form yet still intact. With nothing extra. Sometimes the ornamentation can be of use, often not. Less is generally more.

If you have two units you want to put together, whether it be two sentences or two parts of a song, there can be a tremendous amount of power in doing so without using a transition. Try finding the simplest, most elegant way to put a point across, with the least amount of information.

If there's any question as to whether an element serves the piece, it's probably a good idea to let it go. Some artists get superstitious about removing aspects of a work, as if it will make the project evaporate before their eyes. So it's worth remembering that anything taken away can always be put back later, if needed.

> Perfection is finally obtained not when there is no longer anything to add, but when there's no longer anything to take away.
> —Antoine de Saint-Exupéry, *Wind, Sand and Stars*

In the end,
the sum total of the essence
of our individual works
may serve as a reflection.
The closer we get
to the true essence of each work,
the sooner they will somehow,
at some point in time,
provide clues as to our own.

Apocrypha

$$\odot$$

Every artist has heroes.

Creators whose work we connect with, whose methods we aspire to, whose words we cherish. These exceptional talents can seem beyond human, like mythological figures.

From a distance, what can we know to be true?

Without witnessing a beloved work's actual creation, it's impossible to know what truly happened. And if we did observe the process with our own eyes, our account would be an outside interpretation at best.

The stories about how works get made and the rituals of the artists who make them are generally exaggerated, and often pure fiction.

A work of art happens naturally, of its own accord. We may wonder where the underlying idea came from and how each individual element was put together to produce such a masterwork. But nobody knows how or why these things happen. Often, not even the maker.

In cases when the artist thinks they know, their interpretation may not be accurate or the whole story.

We live in a mysterious world full of uncertainties. And we regularly make assumptions to explain them. Coming to terms with the complexity of our human experience allows us to exit our natural state of confusion. To survive.

Generally our explanations are guesses. These vague hypotheticals become fixed in our minds as fact. We are interpretation machines, and this process of labeling and detaching is efficient but not accurate. We are the unreliable narrators of our own experience.

So when an artist creates a work that comes together by an unseen hand, and the process is later analyzed, what we get is more storytelling. This is art history. Art reality is forever unknown.

These stories may be interesting and fun to think about. But to believe a specific method is responsible for the quality of a work is misleading. Especially if it causes you to repeat that process in hopes of achieving a similar result.

Legendary figures in art and history are sometimes held up as deities. It is counterproductive to measure ourselves against them because they never existed as such. They are beings with typical human vulnerabilities and flaws just like us.

Each artist works with their own balance of strengths and weaknesses. And there is no rule that more praiseworthy strengths or romanticized self-destruction equals better art. Expressing yourself is all that matters.

All art is a form of poetry. It's always changing, never fixed. We may think we know what a piece we made means, yet over time that interpretation may change. The creator stops being the creator once they finish the work. They then become the viewer. And the viewer can bring as much of their own meaning to a piece as the creator.

We will never know a work's true meaning. It's helpful to remember that there are forces at work beyond our comprehension. Let's make art, and let others make the stories.

We are dealing in a magic realm.
Nobody knows why or how it works.

Tuning Out
(Undermining Voices)

We may take years, even decades, to create our first project. It typically develops in a vacuum, in an ordinary way, in a conversation mostly with ourselves.

After we share it, outside influences can emerge. An audience appears, whether it consists of friends or large groups of strangers. Individuals and companies with business interests can sign on. And as we begin to work on our next project, loud outer voices may speak at us from the sidelines, influencing us in different creative directions. Demanding the work now, without concern for quality.

As these voices enter an artist's head—concern for deadlines, deals, sales, media attention, public image, staff, overhead, growing the audience, keeping the existing fan base—they can undermine our focus. The intention of our art can shift from self-expression to self-sustainment. From creative choices to business decisions.

The key to navigating this phase of an artistic journey is learning to tune out. To prevent external pressures from entering our inner process and interfering with the pure creative state.

It helps to recall the clear mindset that produced the first work and allowed success to happen originally.

Set aside not just business concerns, but the needs and thoughts of these outside voices. Keep them out of your consciousness while in pursuit of your best work.

When you're able to focus purely on creativity and work in a sacred space, everyone benefits. And all other priorities are served.

⊙

At any stage in a career, the critic in your head may make its voice heard. Repeating that you're not talented enough. Your idea isn't good enough. Art isn't a worthwhile investment of your time. The result won't be well-received. You're a failure.

Or there may be a contrary voice that tells you that everything you do is perfect and you will be the greatest phenomenon the world has ever seen.

More often than not, these are outer voices that were absorbed early in life. Perhaps a critical or doting parent, teacher, or mentor. These voices are not our own. We have internalized someone else's judgment. So it can be met with the same indifference as the other random chatter.

Any pressure you feel around the work—from the inside or outside—is a signal for self-examination. The artist's goal is to keep themselves pure and unattached. To avoid letting stress, responsibility, fear, and dependence on a particular outcome distract. And if it does, it's never too late to reset.

The first step of clearing is acknowledgment. Notice yourself feeling the weight of self-criticism or the pressure to live up to expectations. And remember that commercial success is completely out of your control. All that matters is that you are making something you love, to the best of your ability, here and now.

Working to free yourself from inner voices is a kind of meditation. Set aside all concerns for a stretch of time and say, I'm only going to focus on this one practice: making great work.

If any distractions come along during that period, don't ignore them or focus on them. Don't give them any energy at all. Let them pass, like clouds parting around a mountain.

Regularly engaging in this practice builds the muscle of focused intention, which you can use in everything you do. Eventually, tuning out the undermining voices and losing yourself in the work will not be an effort of will, but an earned ability.

Self-Awareness

$$\bigodot$$

As children, few of us are taught to understand and prioritize our feelings. For the most part, the educational system doesn't ask us to access our sensitivity, but to be obedient. To do what is expected. Our natural independent spirit is tamed. Free thought is constrained. There is a set of rules and expectations put upon us that is not about exploring who we are or what we're capable of.

The system is not here for our benefit. It holds us back as individuals to support its own continued existence. This is particularly undermining to independent thinking and free expression. As artists, our mission is not to fit in or conform to popular thinking. Our purpose is to value and develop our understanding of ourselves and the world around us.

To be self-aware is to have the ability to tune in to what we think, how we feel, and how much we feel it without interference. To notice how we notice the outside world.

A well-tuned ability to expand and refine our self-awareness is the key to making revelatory works. Sometimes there are many versions of pretty good. How do we know when we arrive at greatness?

Self-awareness allows us to listen to what's going on in the body, and notice the energetic changes that either pull us forward or push us away. Sometimes they are subtle, other times intense.

Our definition of self-awareness as artists relates directly to the way we tune in to our inner experience, not the way we are externally perceived. The more we identify with our self as it exists through the eyes of others, the more disconnected we become and the less energy we have to draw from.

We extend our reach for a higher consciousness. Releasing attachment to our perceived self and limitations. We are seeking not to define ourselves, but to expand ourselves, to tune in to our limitlessness nature and connection to all that is.

Self-awareness is a transcendence. An abandonment of ego. A letting go.

This notion may seem elusive, because in the same breath, it includes tuning in to the self and surrendering the self. Yet these are not as contradictory as they may seem. As artists, we are on a continual quest to get closer to the universe by getting closer to self. Moving ever nearer to the point where we can no longer tell where one begins and the other ends. We're on a distant metaphysical journey from the here to the now.

It's helpful to work as if the project you're engaged in is bigger than you.

Right Before Our Eyes

(·)

Artists occasionally experience a sense of stagnation. A block. This isn't because the flow of creativity has stopped. It can't. This generative energy is ceaseless. It may just be that we are choosing not to engage with it.

Think of an artistic impasse as another type of creation. A block of your own making. A decision, conscious or unconscious, not to participate in the stream of productive energy that is available to us at all times.

When we feel constricted, we might begin to create an opening through surrender. If we let go of our analytical thoughts, the flow might be able to find a path through us more easily. We can be and do, rather than think and try. Create in the present, rather than anticipating the future.

Each time we surrender, we may come to find that the answer we seek is right before our eyes. A new idea arises. An object in the room inspires. Feelings in the body amplify.

This is worth considering in difficult moments when we appear to be stuck, to have lost our way, to have nothing left to give.

What if this is all a story?

Be mindful not to abandon a project prematurely because you have given in to all-or-nothing thinking. I have witnessed several artists start projects and throw them away for this very reason. It's easy to create a piece, recognize a flaw, and want to discard the entire work. This reflex happens in all areas of life.

When you look at the work, practice truly seeing what's there, without a negativity bias. Be open to seeing both strength and weakness, instead of focusing on the weakness and allowing it to overwhelm the strength. You might come to realize 80 percent of the work is quite good, and if the other 20 percent fits in just the right way, the work becomes magnificent. This is far better than trashing the work because one small part isn't a perfect fit. When you acknowledge a weakness, always consider how it could either be removed or improved before discarding the entire piece.

What if the source of creativity is always there, knocking patiently on the doors of our perception, waiting for us to unbolt the locks?

If you are open and stay tuned
to what's happening,
the answers will be revealed.

A Whisper Out of Time

It is common for an artist to question the weight of their ideas.

A five-year-long creative process might have begun with a fleeting moment in a dream or a remark overheard in a parking lot. In hindsight, this tiny seed that led us down a winding path may seem insignificant. We might wonder if it's big enough or if the direction is important enough to keep traveling.

When gathering seeds to begin our work, we may be tempted to look for a grand sign before committing ourselves. A clap of thunder to assure us that we've found the right path. We may discard ideas that don't seem of great importance or magnitude.

But the size does not matter. Volume does not equal value.

We can't weigh Source material based on the initial impact it makes on arrival. Sometimes the smallest seed grows into the biggest tree. The most innocent idea can lead to the most consequential writing. Trivial insights can open the doors to vast new worlds. The most delicate message could be of the greatest importance.

Even if the seed is nothing more than what we notice—a momentary perception, an unexpected thought, even the echo of a memory—it's enough.

Most often, the hints of inspiration and direction from Source are small. They appear as tiny signals traveling through the void of space, quiet and subtle, like a whisper.

⊙

To hear whispers, the mind must also be quiet. We pay close attention on all fronts. Our antennae sensitively tuned.

Boosting our receptivity may require a relaxing of effort. If we're trying to solve a problem, *trying* can get in the way. Splashing in a pond stirs up clouds of dirt in the clear water. In relaxing the mind, we may have greater clarity to hear the whisper when it comes.

In addition to meditation, we might softly hold on to a

question and go for a walk, swim, or drive. The question isn't being worked on, just loosely held in awareness. We are posing it gently to the Universe and opening ourselves to receive an answer.

Sometimes the words seem to arise from the outside, and other times, the inside. Whatever route the information arrives through, we allow it to come by grace, not effort. The whisper cannot be wrestled into existence, only welcomed with an open state of mind.

Expect a Surprise

If we're paying attention, we may notice that some of our most interesting artistic choices come about by accident. Springing from moments of communion with the work, when the self disappears. Sometimes they feel like mistakes.

These mistakes are the subconscious engaged in problem-solving. They're a kind of creative Freudian slip, where a deeper part of you overrides your conscious intention and offers an elegant solution. When asked how it happened, you may say that you don't know. It just came through you in the moment.

In time, we grow accustomed to experiencing moments that are difficult to explain. Moments where you give the art exactly what it needs, without intending to, where a solution seems as if it appeared without your intervention at all.

In time, we learn to count on the hand of the unknown.

For some artists, being surprised is a rare experience. But it's possible to cultivate this gift through invitation.

One way is through letting go of control. Release all expectations about what the work will be. Approach the process with humility and the unexpected will visit more often. Many of us are taught to create through sheer will. If we choose surrender, the ideas that want to come through us will not be blocked.

It's similar to writing a book by following a detailed outline. Set aside the outline, write with no map, and see what happens. The premise you start with could develop into something more. Something you couldn't have planned and would never have arisen if you were locked into following a particular script.

With your intention set, and the destination unknown, you are free to surrender your conscious mind, dive into the raging stream of creative energy, and watch the unexpected appear, again and again.

As each small surprise leads to another, you'll soon find the biggest surprise:
You learn to trust yourself—in the universe, with the universe, as a unique channel to a higher wisdom.

This intelligence is beyond our understanding. Through grace, it is accessible to all.

Living in discovery is at all times preferable to living through assumptions.

Great Expectations

$$\odot$$

When beginning a new project, we're often met with anxiety. It visits almost all of us no matter how experienced, successful, or well-prepared we might be.

In facing the void, there is a tension of opposites. There is an excitement for the possibility something great may be realized and a dread it might not. And the result is out of our control.

The weight of our expectations can grow heavy. As does the fear that we are not up to the task at hand. What if we can't pull it off this time?

What helps to keep these worries at bay and move forward is a trust in the process.

When we sit down to work, remember that the outcome is out of our control. If we are willing to take each step into the unknown with grit and determination, carrying with us all of our collected knowledge, we will ultimately get to where we're going. This destination may not be one we've chosen in advance. It will likely be more interesting.

This isn't a matter of blind belief in yourself. It's a matter of experimental faith.

You work not as an evangelist, expecting miracles, but as a scientist, testing and adjusting and testing again. Experimenting and building on the results. Faith is rewarded, perhaps even more than talent or ability.

After all, how can we offer the art what it needs without blind trust? We are required to believe in something that doesn't exist in order to allow it to come into being.

⊙

When we don't yet know where we're going, we don't wait. We move forward in the dark. If nothing we attempt yields progress, we rely on belief and will. We may take several steps backward in the sequence to move ahead.

If we try ten experiments and none of them work, we have a choice. We can take it personally, and think of ourselves as a failure and question our ability to solve the problem. Or we can recognize we've ruled out ten ways that don't work, bringing us that much closer to a solution. For the artist, whose job is testing possibilities, success is as much ruling out a solution as finding one that works.

In the process of experimentation, we allow ourselves to make mistakes, to go too far, to go even further, to be inept. There is no failure, as every step we take is necessary to reach our destination, including the missteps. Each experiment is valuable in its own way if we learn something from it. Even if we can't comprehend its worth, we are still practicing our craft, moving ever so much closer to mastery.

With unshakable faith, we work under the assumption that the problem is already solved. The answer is out there, perhaps it's obvious. We just haven't come across it yet.

Over time, as you complete more projects, this faith in experimentation grows. You're able to hold high expectations, move forward with patience, and trust the mysterious unfolding before you. With the understanding that the process will get you where you're going. Wherever that reveals itself to be. And the magical nature of the unfolding never ceases to take our breath away.

Sometimes the mistakes
are what makes a work great.
Humanity breathes in mistakes.

Openness

Our minds seek rules and limits. In attempting to navigate a large, uncertain world, we develop beliefs that give us a coherent framework, reduced options, and a false sense of certainty.

Before civilization, the natural world was far more dangerous. In order for humans to survive, we had to assess situations and parse information quickly.

This survival instinct persists today. With the overwhelming amount of information available to us, we are more reliant than ever on categorization, labeling, and shortcuts. Few have the time and expertise to evaluate each new choice with a completely open, unbiased mind. There is also a sense of security in shrinking our world to make it more manageable.

The artist does not value safety and smallness. Reducing our palette to fit the perimeter of limited beliefs suppresses the work. New creative possibilities and sources of inspiration are blocked from view. If an artist keeps playing the same note, eventually the audience loses interest.

There's a dullness in sameness. At a certain point in the creator's journey, the mind can become more resistant to new methods or new styles of expression. A once-useful routine might, over time, turn into a narrow, fixed way of working. To break out of this mindset, our charge is to soften, to become more porous, and to let more light in.

To keep the artistic output evolving, continually replenish the vessel from which it comes. And actively stretch your point of view.

Invite beliefs that are different from the ones you hold and try to see beyond your own filter. Purposely experiment past the boundaries of your taste. Examine approaches you may dismiss as too highbrow or lowbrow. What can we learn from these extremes? What are the unexpected surprises? What closed door might open in your work?

Consider expanding this practice to relationships as well. When a collaborator's feedback or method seems questionable and conflicts with your default setting, reframe this as an exciting opportunity. Do all you can to see from their perspective and understand their point of view, instead of defending your own. In addition to solving the problem at hand, you may uncover something new about yourself and become aware of the limits boxing you in.

The heart of open-mindedness is curiosity. Curiosity doesn't take sides or insist on a single way of doing things. It explores all perspectives. Always open to new ways, always seeking to arrive at original insights. Craving constant expansion, it looks upon the outer limits of the mind with wonder. It pushes to expose falsely set boundaries and break through to new frontiers.

⊙

When we encounter an artistic problem, the reason it's a problem is typically because it conflicts with our accepted beliefs of what is and isn't possible. Or our expectations for what is expected to happen.

A song may begin to veer away from our assumed genre. A painter might run out of a certain type of paint. A film director might experience a malfunction with a piece of equipment on set.

When something doesn't go according to plan, we have a choice to either resist it or incorporate it.

Instead of shutting the project down or expressing frustration, we might consider what else can be done with the materials at hand. What solutions can be improvised? How can the flow be redirected?

There may be a beneficial purpose behind the issue at hand. The universe could be leading us to an even better solution.

There's no way to know.

We can only flow with the challenges as they come and keep an open mind, with no baggage, no previous story to live up to. We simply begin from a neutral place, allow the process to unfold, and welcome the winds of change to guide the way.

Many people may seem walled off.
But sometimes walls can provide
different ways of seeing
over and around obstacles.

Surrounding the Lightning Bolt

(•)

An explosion of information arrives in inspired moments. How can we avoid becoming fixated on these bolts of lightning? Some artists live as storm chasers awaiting spontaneous strikes, longing for the thrill.

A more constructive strategy is to focus less on the lightning bolt and more on the spaces surrounding it. The space before, because lightning does not strike unless the right preconditions are met, and the space after, because the electricity dissipates if you do not capture it and use it. When we are struck by an epiphany, our experience of what's possible has been expanded. In that instant, we are broken open. We've entered a new reality. Even when we leave that heightened state, the experience sometimes remains in us. Other times it's fleeting.

If lightning should strike, and this information is channeled through the aether to us, what follows is a great deal of practical work. While we can't command a lightning bolt's arrival, we can control the space around it. We accomplish this by preparing beforehand and honoring our obligation to it afterward.

If lightning doesn't strike, our work need not be delayed. Some storm chasers believe that inspiration precedes creation. This is not always the case. Working without lightning bolts is simply working. Like carpenters, we show up each day and do our job. Sculptors knead clay, sweep the studio floor, and lock up for the night. Graphic designers sit at their workstations, select images, choose fonts, create layouts, and hit *save*.

Artists are ultimately craftspeople. Sometimes our ideas come through bolts of lightning. Other times only through effort, experiment, and craft. As we work, we may notice connections and become surprised by the wonder of what's revealed through the doing itself. In a way, these small a-ha! moments are also bolts of lightning. Less vivid, they still illuminate our way.

⊙

A lightning bolt may just be a temporary phenomenon, a momentary expression of cosmic potential. Not every inspired idea is destined to become a great work of art. Sometimes lightning arrives and we have no use for it. A moment of inspiration may excite us to begin a long exploration to discover its practical form, only to arrive at a dead end.

The only way to find out is to engage wholeheartedly in the work. Without diligence, inspiration alone rarely yields work of much consequence. In some projects, inspiration can be minimal and effort takes over. In others, inspiration can strike and the effort needed to manifest its potential can't be summoned.

Making great art may not always require great effort, but without it, you'll never know. If inspiration calls, we ride the lightning until the energy is exhausted.

The ride may not last long. But we are grateful for the opportunity. If inspiration does not come to lead the way, we show up anyway.

Do what you can
with what you have.
Nothing more is needed.

24/7
(Staying In It)

(•)

The artist's job is never truly finished.

In many occupations, when we go home, we leave our work behind at the office. The artist is always on call. Even after we get up from hours engaged in our craft, the clock is still running.

This is because the artist's job is of two kinds:

The work of doing.

The work of being.

Creativity is something you are, not only something you do. It's a way of moving through the world, every minute, every day. If you're not driven to an unrealistic standard of dedication, it may not be the path for you. So much of the artist's work is about balance, so it's ironic that this way of life leaves little room for it.

Once you acquiesce to the demands of the creative life, it becomes a part of you. Even in the midst of a project, you still look for new ideas each day. At any moment, you're prepared to stop what you're doing to make a note or a drawing, or capture a fleeting thought. It becomes second nature. And we're always in it, every hour of the day.

Staying in it means a commitment to remain open to what's around you. Paying attention and listening. Looking for connections and relationships in the outside world. Searching for beauty. Seeking stories. Noticing what you find interesting, what makes you lean forward. And knowing all of this is available to use next time you sit down to work, where the raw data gets put into form.

There is no telling where that next great story, painting, recipe, or business idea is going to come from. Just as a surfer can't control the waves, artists are at the mercy of the creative rhythms of nature. This is why it's of such great importance to remain aware and present at all times. Watching and waiting.

Maybe the best idea
is the one you're going to
come up with this evening.

Spontaneity
(Special Moments)

The song that springs to mind fully formed.
The impulsive windings of a Jackson Pollock.
The spontaneous dance move that fills the floor.

Artists may prize spontaneous works, thinking there is some higher purity or specialness held in works channeled instead of carefully planned.

But can you tell the difference between art that sprang to mind and art that was crafted with forethought? And what does this difference matter?

Art made accidentally has no more or less weight than art created through sweat and struggle.

Whether it took months or minutes does not matter. Quality isn't based on the amount of time invested. So long as what emerges is pleasing to us, the work has fulfilled its purpose.

The story of spontaneity can be misleading. We don't see all the practice and preparation that goes into priming an artist for the spontaneous event to come through. Every work contains a lifetime of experience.

Great artists often labor to make their work appear effortless. Sometimes they might spend years meticulously crafting and refining a composition to appear as if it was made in a day or in a moment.

There are others who romanticize planning and preparation. To them, a spontaneous work has less validity. It seems more like a product of an artist's good fortune than talent.

Consider neutrality. Just do the work and see what comes. If you like a result, accept it graciously, whether it arrives in a sudden flash or after long bouts of difficult, skilled labor.

For some artists, the work comes easily. Bob Dylan could write a song in minutes while Leonard Cohen sometimes took years. And we may love the songs equally.

There's no pattern or logic to this enigmatic process. Not all projects are the same, no two people are the same. The project is the guide we follow. And each comes with its own conditions and requirements.

⊙

If you are an artist whose process is intellectually based, it may be of benefit to play with spontaneity as a tool, a window to discovery and an access point to new parts of yourself.

Attachment to any specific creative process can seal the door through which spontaneity enters. Even if for a short time, it may be of benefit to leave this door cracked open. We can make an experiment of surrender to allow the surprise of discovery to come.

If you sit down to write with no preparation or forethought, you might bypass the conscious mind and draw from the unconscious. You may find that what emerges holds a charge that cannot be duplicated through rational means.

This approach is at the heart of some forms of jazz. When musicians are improvising a piece, preconceived ideas of what to play can prevent the performance from taking flight. The goal is to be in it and allow the music to essentially play itself, accepting the risks. The performances will be good on a good night and bad on a bad night. And perhaps the best jazz musicians are the ones who have the ability to create special moments on a fairly consistent basis. Even spontaneity gets better with practice.

You may worry that a great idea could get lost or overlooked in the spontaneity of a moment. To guard against that when I'm working with an artist, I make an endless amount of notes. When outside observers come into the studio, they often can't believe how clinical the process looks. They imagine a big music party. But we're constantly generating detailed notes on focus points and experiments to test. For almost everything that's said, someone is writing it down. Two weeks later, there will come a time when someone will ask a question like: What was that lyric we loved? What was the previous version of that element like? Which take was the best for the fill going into the second chorus? And we go back to the notes.

There's a great volume of material constantly being generated, and we're so in the moment that it's impossible to remember everything, even something that happened seconds ago. By the time we get to the end of the song, I'm absorbed in listening, and those thoughts are gone. Faithful note-taking by a connected observer helps prevent special moments from getting lost in the churn of excitement.

Sometimes,
it can be the most ordinary moment
that creates an extraordinary piece of art.

How to Choose

(•)

Every piece of art consists of a series of choices, like a tree with many branches.

Our work begins with a seed, which sprouts a trunk of the core idea. As it grows, each decision we make becomes a branch splitting off in a new direction, growing finer and finer in detail as we move further out.

At each fork, we can go in any number of directions, and our choice will alter the final result. Often radically.

How do we decide which direction to take? How can we know which choice will lead us to the best possible version of the work?

The answer is rooted in a universal principle of relationships. We can only tell where something is in relation to something else. And we can only assess an object or principle if we have something to compare and contrast it to. Otherwise it's an absolute beyond evaluation.

We can hack into this principle to improve our creations through A/B testing. It is difficult to assess a work or a choice on its own without another point of reference. If you place two options side by side and make a direct comparison, our preferences become clear.

We limit our options for each test to two choices wherever possible. Any more cloud the process. When cooking a dish, we might taste two different varieties of the same ingredient before deciding which to use. Two actors reading the same monologue, two shades of a color, or two different floor plans of an apartment.

We place them next to each other, step back, and directly compare. More often than not, there will be a clear draw toward one.

If there isn't, we quiet ourselves to see which has a subtle pull. Following the natural feedback in the body, we move toward the option that hints at the ecstatic.

Whenever possible, make the A/B test blind. Conceal as many details as possible about each option to remove any biases undermining fair comparison. For example, some musicians have a preference for either analog or digital recording. It is worth recording using both methods, then

306

devising a way to listen to each without any indication of which is which. Sometimes the artists are surprised by their preference.

If you're at an impasse in an A/B test, consider the coin toss method. Decide which option will be heads and which will be tails, then flip the coin. When the coin is spinning in the air, you'll likely notice a quiet preference or wish for one of the two to come up. Which are you rooting for? This is the option to go with. It's the one the heart desires. The test is over before the coin ever lands.

When testing, don't overintellectualize your choice of criteria. You're looking for that first instinct, the knee-jerk reaction before any thought. The instinctual tug tends to be the purest, whereas the second, more reasoned thought tends to be processed and distorted through analysis.

The goal is to turn off the conscious mind and follow our impulses. Children are exceptionally good at this. They may move through several different spontaneous expressions of emotion in a single minute, without judgment or attachment. As we grow older, we're taught to hide or bury these reactions. This mutes our inner sensitivity.

If we were to learn anything, it would be to free ourselves from any beliefs or baggage or dogma that gets in the way of us acting according to our true nature. The closer we get to a childlike state of free self-expression, the purer our test and the better our art.

⊙

Once a work is complete, no amount of testing can guarantee we've made the best possible version. These qualities are not measurable. We test to identify which is the best version from the options at hand.

No matter what route you take, if you complete the journey, you will reach the same destination. This destination is a work we feel energized to share. One we look back on and wonder in amazement how it could have come from us.

Shades and Degrees

In the creation of art, proportions can be deceptive.

Two seeds of inspiration might seem indistinguishable, but one may yield volumes and the other little to nothing. What begins as a lightning bolt may not produce a work that reflects its initial magnitude, whereas a humble spark may grow into an epic masterpiece.

In crafting, the amount of time we put in and the results we get are rarely in balance. A large movement may materialize all at once; other times a tiny detail may take days. And there's no predicting how much of a role either will play in the final outcome.

Another surprising facet of the process is how the tiniest

of details can clearly define a work. They can determine whether a piece is stimulating or languid, finished or unfinished. We make one dab of the brush, one tweak in the mix—and suddenly the work jumps from being halfway done to complete. When it happens, this seems miraculous.

What ultimately makes a work great is the sum total of the tiniest details. From start to finish, everything has shades and degrees. There is no fixed scale. There can't be, because sometimes the smallest elements are the ones that weigh the most.

When the work has five mistakes,
it's not yet completed.
When it has eight mistakes,
it might be.

Implications
(Purpose)

◉

You may sometimes wonder: Why am I doing this? What's it all for?

Questions such as these come early and often for some. Others seem to go their whole lives without ever troubling themselves with these thoughts. Maybe they know that the maker and the explainer are always two different people, even when they're the same person.

In the end, these questions are of little importance. There doesn't need to be a purpose guiding what we choose to make. When examined more closely, we might find this grandiose idea useless. It implies we know more than we can know.

If we like what we are creating, we don't have to know why. Sometimes the reasons are obvious, sometimes not. And they can change over time. It could be good for any of a thousand different reasons. When we're making things we love, our mission is accomplished. There's nothing at all to figure out.

Think to yourself:
I'm just here to create.

Freedom

⊙

Does the artist have a social responsibility?

Some might agree with this notion and want to encourage artists to create accordingly.

Those who hold this belief may not have a clear understanding of the function of art in society and its integral social value.

The work of art serves its purpose independent of the creator's interest in social responsibility. Wanting to change people's minds about an issue or have an effect on society may interfere with the quality and purity of the work.

This doesn't mean that our work can't have those qualities, but we generally don't get there by planning them. In the creative process, it's often more difficult to accomplish a goal by aiming at it.

Deciding what to say in advance doesn't allow whatever's best to come. Meaning is assigned once an inspired idea is followed through.

It's best to wait until a work is complete to discover what it is saying. Holding your work hostage to meaning is a limitation.

Works that attempt to overtly preach a message often don't connect as hoped, while a piece not intended to address a societal ill may become an anthem for a revolutionary cause.

Art is far more powerful than our plans for it.

⊙

Art can't be irresponsible. It speaks to all aspects of the human experience.

There are sides of ourselves that aren't welcome in polite society, thoughts and feelings too dark to share. When we recognize them expressed in art, we feel less alone.

More real, more human.

This is the therapeutic power of making and consuming art.

Art is above and beyond judgment. It either speaks to you or it doesn't.

The artist's only responsibility is to the work itself. There are no other requirements. You're free to create what you will.

You don't have to stand for your work, nor does your work have to stand for anything but itself. You are not a symbol of it. Nor is it necessarily symbolic of you. It will be interpreted and reinterpreted in the eyes and ears of those who know almost nothing about you.

If there were anything you might stand for, it would be to defend this creative autonomy. Not just from outside censors, but from the voices in your head that have internalized what's considered acceptable. The world is only as free as it allows its artists to be.

What we say,
what we sing,
what we paint—
we get to choose.

We have no responsibility
to anything other than the art itself.
The art is the final word.

The Possessed

(•)

Artists are often portrayed in films and books as tortured geniuses. Starving, self-destructive, dancing on the brink of madness.

This has instilled the belief that to make art, one has to be broken. Or that the force of art is so powerful that it breaks its maker.

Neither generalization is true. These misconceptions have a disheartening effect on the would-be artist. Some creators may live with a profound darkness. Others stride forward with ease and exuberance. Between lies a wide range of artistic temperament.

For those called to art who do struggle with an overwhelming sensitivity, the creative process can have a therapeutic power. It offers a sense of deep connection. A safe place to voice the unspeakable and bare their soul. In these cases, art does not unravel the maker, but makes them whole.

Although the character of the tortured artist tends to live more in mythology than in reality, this does not mean that art comes easily. It requires the obsessive desire to create great things. This pursuit doesn't have to be agonizing. It can be enlivening. It's up to you.

Whether you have a powerful passion or a tortured compulsion, neither makes the art any better or worse. If you are able to choose between these paths, consider selecting the more sustainable one. An artist earns the title simply through self-expression, as they work in their own way at their own pace.

What Works for You
(Believing)

There's a songwriter who wrote all of her music in the same messy room in an old office building. It hasn't been touched in thirty years and she refuses to let it be cleaned. The secret is in that room, she says.

She believes it, and it works for her.

Charles Dickens carried a compass to make sure he always slept facing north. He believed that alignment with the electrical currents of the Earth supported his creativity. Dr. Seuss had a bookcase with a false door hiding hundreds of unusual hats. He and his editor would each pick a hat and stare at each other until inspiration came.

These stories may or may not be completely true. It

doesn't matter. If a ritual or superstition has a positive effect on an artist's work, then it's worth pursuing.

Artists have created in every way possible—at the extremes of chaos and order, and at the meeting point of different methods at once. There is no right time, right strategy, or right equipment.

It may be helpful to receive advice from more experienced artists, but as information, not as prescription. It can open you to another point of view and broaden your idea of what's possible.

Established artists generally draw from their personal experience and recommend the solutions that worked for them. These tend to be specific to their journey, not yours. It's worth remembering that their way is not *the* way.

Your path is unique, for only you to follow. There is no single route to great art.

This doesn't mean ignore the wisdom of others. Receive wisdom skillfully. Try it on for size and see how it fits. Incorporate what's useful. Let go of the rest. And no matter how credible the source, test and tune in to yourself to discover what works for you.

The only practice that matters is the one you consistently do, not the practice of any other artist. Find your most generative method, apply it, and then let it go when it is no longer of use. There is no wrong way to make art.

Adaptation

Something peculiar happens when we practice.

With a piece of music we're learning, for example, we might play it over and over. It gets a little easier, a little harder, a little easier. Then we stop and come back a day or two later, and suddenly it flows from us far more naturally. Our fingers seem to have more agility. A difficult knot has untied itself.

This phenomenon is different from most forms of learning. It's not reading information and remembering it. It's more mysterious than that. You wake up one morning, transported to this new reality where you suddenly have more skill than you did before you went to sleep. The body has changed, adapting to the task it was presented and rising to perform it.

Practice gets us part of the way there. Then it takes time for practice to be absorbed into the body. We might call this the recovery phase. In weightlifting, the practice breaks down muscle and recovery builds it back stronger than before. The passive element of practice is as important as the active one.

It's commonly thought that achieving artistic mastery means working tirelessly. This is true. But it's only half of it. There may be benefit in taking breaks, in stepping away and returning at a later point. Whether when practicing your instrument or over the course of your life's work, recovery at the opportune time will cause greater leaps in improvement.

This cycle of practice and adaptation creates multifaceted growth. You are building concentration and focus, and training your brain to learn more effectively. More easily.

As a result, other skills are lifted as well. Teaching yourself to play piano will likely improve your hearing. And you may well get better at math.

$$\odot$$

This adaptation process plays a still bigger role. One beyond learning. It's an aspect of the universe manifesting through us. A will to life.

An idea gathers energy, building charge, yearning to be embraced. We can hear it, see it, imagine it, but it may be an inch further away than we can currently reach. As we trace back over it, again and again, more and more detail comes into focus and we become wholly consumed.

Our capacity grows and stretches to touch the idea that Source is offering up. We accept this responsibility with gratitude, cherish it, and protect it. Acknowledging with humility that it comes from beyond us. More important than us. And not just for us. We are in its service.

This is why we are here. It is the impulse through which humanity evolves. We adapt and grow in order to receive. These inherent abilities made it possible for humans, and for all life, over eons, to survive and thrive in an ever-changing world. And to play our predestined role in advancing the cycle of creation. Supporting the birth of other new and more complex forms. If we choose to participate.

Translation

Art is an act of decoding. We receive intelligence from Source, and interpret it through the language of our chosen craft.

In all fields, there are different degrees of fluency. Our level of skill influences our ability to best articulate this translation, in the same way vocabulary affects communication.

This is not a direct correlation. It's a fluid relationship. When learning a new language, you may be able to ask a question, speak a beautifully memorized phrase, or accidentally say something humorous. At the same time, you may feel unable to share bigger ideas, more nuanced feelings, and express the full extent of who you are.

The more we develop, expand, and sharpen our skills, the more fluent we become. We can experience greater freedom and less sameness in the act of making. And vastly improve our ability to manifest the best version of our ideas in the physical world.

For the sake of both the work and our own enjoyment, it's of great value to continue honing our craft. Every artist, at every juncture in the process, can get better through practice, study, and research. The gifts of art are more learned and developed than innate. We can always improve.

As Arn Anderson once noted: "I'm both a professor and student, because if you're no longer a student, you don't have the right to call yourself a professor."

If you feel unable to hit a note or faithfully paint an image, it's helpful to remember that the challenge is not that you can't do it, but that you haven't done it *yet*. Avoid thinking in impossibilities. If there's a skill or piece of knowledge you need for a particular project, you can do the homework and work toward it over time. You can train for anything.

While this framework will broaden your ability, it won't guarantee you become a great artist. A guitarist could play the most complex solo and while technically impressive, it might not connect emotionally, while an amateur could perform a simplistic three-chord song and move you to tears.

At the same time, there's no need to fear learning too much theory. It won't undermine the pure expression of your voice. If you don't let it. Having the knowledge won't hurt the work. How you *use* the knowledge may. You have new tools. You don't have to use them.

Learning provides more ways to reliably convey your ideas. From our enlarged menu, we can still choose the simplest, most elegant option. Painters like Barnett Newman, Piet Mondrian, and Joseph Albers were classically trained, and they chose to spend their careers exploring simple, monochromatic, geometric shapes.

Consider your craft as an energy alive in you. It's just as much a part of the cycle of evolution as other living things are. It wants to grow. It wants to flower.

To hone your craft is to honor creation. It doesn't matter if you become the best in your field. By practicing to improve, you are fulfilling your ultimate purpose on this planet.

Clean Slate

After spending thousands of hours working on a piece, it's difficult to judge it from a neutral place. When someone experiences the work for the first time, after only two minutes they may see it more clearly than you do.

In time, almost every artist finds themselves too close to the things they make. After endlessly working on the same piece, perspective is lost. We develop a kind of blindness. Doubt and disorientation may creep in. Judgment is impaired.

If we train ourselves to step away from the work, to truly

detach from it, to distract ourselves completely, to dive fully into something else . . .

After being away for a long enough period of time, when we come back, we just may be able to see it as if for the first time.

This is the practice of cleaning the slate. The ability to create as an artist and experience the work as a first-time viewer, dropping baggage from the past of what you thought you wanted the work to be. The mission is to be in the present moment with the work.

Here is one concrete example of keeping a clean slate. The final stage of the recording process is the mix. This is where a sound engineer balances the levels of different instruments to best present the material.

When listening to a mix in progress, I make a list of notes. Maybe the vocal in the bridge isn't loud enough. The drum fill in the transition to the last chorus wants to have more importance. Or we may need to duck a certain instrument in the intro to make space for another event.

A common practice is to make those changes, tick each item off the checklist, and then play back the song with the list in mind. *Okay, are the vocals in the bridge louder as I requested? Yes, check. Does the drum fill in the transition seem more important? Yes, check.*

You're anticipating each part. Selectively paying attention to see if your changes were made, rather than listening to the song as a whole and seeing if it's actually better than it was before.

The ego comes in, saying: *I wanted this to happen, I got what I wanted, so it's a problem solved.*

But this isn't necessarily true. Yes, the changes were made, but did they improve the work? Or have they set off a domino effect that created other problems?

At this stage in the process, every element of a work is interdependent. So even a small change can have unexpected ramifications. When the mix is updated to reflect your list, you may falsely assume you've made progress.

The key is to give the notes to someone else to implement when you can, then discard the list and never refer to it again. When the revised mix is played, listen as if for the first time and begin a new list of notes from scratch. This usually helps to hear things as they truly are and guide your progress to arrive at the best version.

A way to practice keeping a clean slate is to avoid looking at the work too often. If you finish a section or come to a sticking point, consider putting the project away and not engaging with it for a period of time. Let it sit for a minute, a week, or longer, while you go get lost.

Meditation is a valuable tool for hitting the reset button. You may also try vigorous exercise, a scenic adventure, or immersing yourself in an unrelated creative endeavor.

When you return with a clear perspective, you will more

likely have the discernment to see what the project wants and needs.

What allows this to happen is the passing of time. Time is where learning occurs. Unlearning as well.

Context

(•)

Imagine a flower in an open meadow.

Now take the same flower and slip it into the barrel of a
rifle. Or place it on a gravestone. Notice in each case how
you feel. The significance changes. In new surroundings, the
same object can take on considerably different meanings.

The context changes the content.

In your work, consider the implications of this principle.
If you're painting a portrait, the background is part of the
context. Changing the background sheds new light on the
foreground. A dark setting sends a different message than a
light one. A dense environment feels different than a sparse
one. The frame, the room the painting is hung in, the

artwork next to it. All these elements affect the perception of the work.

Some artists choose to control all these factors thoroughly. Others leave them to chance. And some create art that is completely context dependent. Andy Warhol's Brillo boxes, for example. In a grocery store, they're disposable packaging for useful kitchen items. In a museum, they're rare objects of fascination and intrigue.

When sequencing a collection of songs, placing a quiet one next to a loud one affects the way a listener hears them both. After the quiet song, the loud one seems more bombastic.

One musician, I'm told, would add his newest track to a playlist along with the most beloved songs of all time to see if his work stood up in this context. If not, he would set it aside and keep working toward greatness.

The social norms of any time and place are another contextual box that art lives in. The same story of a relationship between two people could play out in Detroit or in Bali, in ancient Rome or in a different dimension. In each case, the story may take on new meaning.

Publish the work one particular year as opposed to another, and the meaning can change again. Current events, cultural trends, other works released concurrently all affect a project's reception. Time is another form of context.

When a piece isn't living up to your expectations, consider changing the context. Look past the principle element, examine the variables around it. Play with different combinations. Place it next to other works. Surprise yourself.

A few common options are:

soft-loud
fast-slow
high-low
close-far
bright-dark
large-small
curved-straight
rough-smooth
before-after
inside-outside
same-different

A new context may create a work more powerful than the one you anticipated. One you never could have imagined before changing one seemingly inconsequential element.

The Energy
(In the Work)

○

What motivates us to work so diligently? What drives us to finish certain pieces and not others?

We would like to think that it's our enthusiasm. A feeling that wells up when in the throes of self-expression.

This energy is not generated by us. We are caught by it. We picked it up from the work. *It* contains the charge. A contagious vitality that pulls us forward.

Works hinting at greatness contain a charge we can feel, like static before a lightning storm. They consume their maker, occupying waking thoughts and dreams. Sometimes they become the artist's reason for living.

The energy feels similar to another force of creation in the world:

Love.

A kinetic draw beyond our rational comprehension.

Early in a project, excitement is the inner voltmeter to watch to help choose which seed to develop. When you're handling a seed and the needle jumps, it indicates that the work is worthy of your attention, your devotion. It holds the potential to sustain your interest and make the effort worthwhile.

As you experiment and craft, more energetic charges are set off as further decisions are made. You catch yourself losing track of time, forgetting to eat, withdrawing from the outside world.

Other times the process is a grind. Minutes pass slowly and you count down the days until the work is complete. A prisoner etching marks on a cell wall.

Remember that the energy in the work isn't always accessible to you. At times, you take a wrong turn and the charge is lost. Or you're so deep in the details that you can't see the bigger picture. Even with the greatest work, it's natural for excitement to wax and wane.

If the work is thrilling one day and isn't for a long while after, you may have experienced a false indicator. When the moments of joy seem like a distant memory and the work feels like an obligation to a past idea, this could mean you've either gone too far or that particular seed wasn't actually ready to germinate yet.

If the energy is depleted, either back up a few steps to tap back into the charge or find a new seed generating excitement. One of the skills an artist develops is the ability to recognize when either they or the work have nothing left to give each other.

All living things are interconnected, depending on one another to survive. A work of art is no different. It generates excitement in you. This commands your attention. And your attention is exactly what's required for it to grow. It's a harmonic, mutually dependent relationship. The creator and the creation rely on each other to thrive.

The call of the artist is to follow the excitement. Where there's excitement, there's energy. And where there is energy, there is light.

The best work
is the work you are excited about.

Ending to Start Anew
(Regeneration)

Carl Jung was obsessed with building a round tower to live, think, and create in. The shape was important because he saw "life in the round as something forever coming into being and passing on."

We are part of a constant, interconnected cycle of birth, death, and regeneration. Our bodies decay into the earth to bring forth new life, our energetic mind is returned to the universe to be repurposed.

Art exists in this same cycle of death and rebirth. We participate in this by completing one project so that we can start anew. As in life, each ending invites a fresh beginning. When consumed with a single work to the degree that we believe it's our life's mission, there's no room for the next one to develop.

While the artist's goal is greatness, it's also to move forward. In service to the next project, we finish the current one. In service to the current project, we finish it so it can be set free into the world.

Sharing art is the price of making it. Exposing your vulnerability is the fee.

Out of this experience comes regeneration, finding freshness within yourself for the next project. And all the ones to follow.

Every artist creates a dynamic history. A living museum of finished objects. One work after another. Begun, completed, released. Begun, completed, released. Over and over again. Each a time stamp commemorating a moment of passage. A moment filled with energy, now forever embodied in a work of art.

A work of art is not an end point in itself.
It's a station on a journey.
A chapter in our lives.
We acknowledge these transitions
by documenting each of them.

Play

$\odot$

Making art is a serious matter.
Harnessing creative energy from Source.
Shepherding ideas into the physical plane.
Participating in the cosmic cycle of creation.
The opposite is also true. Making art is pure play.

Within every artist, there's a child emptying a box of crayons onto the floor, searching for just the right color to draw the sky. It might be violet, olive, or burnt orange.

As artists, we strive to preserve this playfulness throughout the gravity of the enterprise. We embrace both the seriousness of the commitment and the playfulness of being completely free in the making.

Take art seriously without going about it in a serious way.

Seriousness saddles the work with a burden. It misses the playful side of being human. The chaotic exuberance of being present in the world. The lightness of pure enjoyment for enjoyment's sake.

In play, there are no stakes. No boundaries. No right or wrong. No quotas for productivity. It's an uninhibited state where your spirit can run free.

The best ideas arise most often and easily through this relaxed state.

Putting importance on the work too soon stirs up instincts of caution. Instead, we want to break free of the shackles of reality and avoid all forms of creative restraint.

Feel free to experiment. Make messes. Embrace randomness. When playtime is over, our adult aspect might come in to analyze: *What did the kids make today? I wonder if it's any good, and what it could mean.*

Each day is about showing up, building things, breaking them down, experimenting, and surprising ourselves. If a four-year-old loses interest in an activity, they don't try to complete it or force themselves to have fun with it. They just shift gears to a new quest. Another form of play.

Some aspects of the work can get tedious. In those moments, can you reengage with the spirit of the process from early on?

Once, in the studio with an artist, we were working on an up-tempo track. We decided to try it acoustically, which led us to add an interesting overdub. Then we muted everything except the overdub and heard it on its own, which led us in a whole new direction. Each different iteration led to a new version, none of it planned or attached to a preconceived notion.

In the end, a beautiful recording emerged that was nothing like the original vision of the song, and was only possible by allowing what was present to suggest a new possibility. Rather than following a plan, a path was taken blindly.

This can happen every day. Find a clue, follow a lead, remain unattached to what came before. And avoid getting stuck with a decision you made five minutes ago.

Think back to when you were a hopeful beginner, when the tools of your craft were exotic and new. Remember the fascination of learning, the joys of your first steps forward.

This might be the best way to retain the energy that drives the work, and to fall in love with the practice again and again.

Whether the work comes easily through play
or with difficulty through struggle,
the quality of the finished piece is unaffected.

The Art Habit
(Sangha)

⊙

If you're looking for the work to support you, you may be asking too much of it. We create *in service* to art, not for what we can get from art.

You may yearn for success as a way to leave an unfulfilling job and support yourself through your passion. This is a reasonable goal. However if the choice is between making great art and supporting yourself, the art comes first. Consider another way to make a living. Success is harder to come by when your life depends on it.

Art is an unstable career path for most. Financial reward often comes in waves, if at all. Some artists might have a vision for what they want to create, but may feel restrained because they don't believe it will pay the bills. It's okay to have a job that supports your art habit. Doing both is a better way of keeping the work pure.

There are jobs that demand your time but little else. You can protect the art you make by choosing an occupation that gives you mental space to formulate and develop your creative vision of the world.

Content can come from jobs that have nothing to do with your passion. Great ideas often originate from unexpected places. Many memorable songs have been written by people in occupations they didn't like.

Another choice is to seek a living in the field you're passionate about. It may be a gallery, a bookstore, a music studio, or a film set. If no jobs are available close to the action, ask if you can moonlight as an intern.

By choosing to be near what you love, you're offered a glimpse behind the scenes of the craft. You can observe the daily life of professional creators and understand the industry and its infrastructure from the inside. After experiencing how it operates, you will come to know whether this path is worthy of your devotion.

Even if it means taking a pay cut initially, choosing this type of work could lead to unexpected opportunities later.

You can also pursue an unrelated career that provides security while keeping art as a hobby, a hobby that's the most important thing in your life. All paths are of equal merit.

⊙

Whatever you choose, it's helpful to have fellow travelers around you. They don't have to be *like* you, just like-minded in some way. Creativity is contagious. When we spend time with other artistic people, we absorb and exchange a way of thinking, a way of looking at the world. This group can be called a Sangha. Each person in this relationship begins seeing with a different imaginative eye.

It doesn't matter if their art form is the same as or different from yours. It's nourishing to be in a community of people who are enthusiastic about art, who you can have long discussions with, and with whom you can trade feedback on the work.

Being part of an artistic community can be one of the great joys of life.

The Prism of Self

Defining one's true self is not so simple. It may be impossible.

We inhabit many different versions of a changing self. The suggestion to *be yourself* may be too general to be of much use. There's being yourself as an artist, being yourself with your family, being yourself at work, being yourself with friends, being yourself in times of crisis or in times of peace, and being yourself for yourself, when by yourself.

In addition to these environmental variations, we are also always changing within. Our moods, our energy level, the stories we tell ourselves, our prior experiences, how hungry or tired we are: All these variants create a new way of being in each moment.

Depending on who we're with, where we are, and how safe or challenged we feel, we are changing all the time. Moving between different aspects of self.

We may have one aspect that wants to be more bold or subversive, which wrestles with our more agreeable, conflict-avoidant self. There may be a dreamer aspect, aspiring to inhabit vast magnificent worlds, at odds with our pragmatic side that questions our ability to make our dreams real.

There is a constant negotiation occurring between these various aspects. And each time we tune in to a particular one, different choices result, changing the outcome of our work.

In a prism, a single beam of light enters and is broken into an array of colors. The self, too, is a prism. Neutral events enter, and are transformed into a spectrum of feelings, thoughts, and sensations. All this information is processed distinctively by each aspect of self, refracting life's light in its own way, and emitting different shades of art.

For this reason, not every work can reflect all of our selves. Perhaps it's never possible, no matter how hard we try. Instead, we might embrace the prism of self, and keep allowing reality to bend uniquely through us.

Like a kaleidoscope, we can adjust the aperture on our vision and change the results. We may aim to work from one particular aspect, like taking on a character, and create something from our darkest self or our most spiritual self.

Those two works won't be the same, but they both come from us and they would both be true colors.

The more we accept our prismlike nature, the more free we become to create in different colors and the more we trust the inconsistent instincts we hold while making art.

We don't have to know why something is good or wonder if it's the "right" decision or if it reflects us accurately. It is simply the light our prism emits naturally at this moment in time.

Any framework, method, or label
you impose on yourself
is just as likely to be a limitation
as an opening.

Let It Be

First, do no harm.

This credo is the well-known guiding principle of the physician's oath. Consider it a universal precept. If asked to participate in a fellow creator's project, proceed delicately.

In its rough form, an early iteration of a work may hold an extraordinary magic. Above all this is to be protected. When working alongside others, keep the oath front of mind.

Simple recognition of the strengths may be enough to move the project forward. A friend played me his current work asking for input. To my ear there was nothing to be added or changed. In the final mix, I suggested, skip the typical refining of balances and sounds. That standard would only water down a masterpiece. Sometimes the most valuable touch a collaborator can have is no touch at all.

Cooperation

The prism of self reflects an aspect of our being into our work. When more than one prism is applied, unexpected possibilities can be unlocked. Whether the perspectives contrast or complement each other, they combine to create a new vision.

Let's call this Cooperation.

Like awareness, cooperation is a practice. The more skillfully we participate in the process, the more comfortable it becomes.

Cooperation is comparable to the way a jazz ensemble improvises. A handful of collaborators, each with their own original point of view, work together to create a new whole, acting and reacting intuitively in the moment. You can lead the play or allow yourself to be led, enjoying the surprise of the unexpected. You can solo or lay out completely, as best serves the work.

Each time we cooperate, we're exposed to different ways of working and problem-solving, which can inform our creative process going forward.

Cooperation is not to be mistaken for competition. It is not a power struggle to get your way or to be proven right.

Competition serves the ego. Cooperation supports the highest outcome.

Think of cooperation as giving or getting a boost to see over a high wall. There's no power struggle in this act. You are simply finding the best route to a new perspective.

It is a disservice to the project to weigh our contribution to it. Believing an idea is best because it's *ours* is an error of inexperience. The ego demands personal authorship, inflating itself at the expense of the art. It can reject new methods that appear counterintuitive and protect familiar ones.

The best results are found when we're impartial and detached from our own strategies. We all benefit when the best idea is chosen, regardless of whether it's ours or not.

⊙

When I work with artists, we make an agreement:

We continue the process until reaching the point where

we are *all* happy with the work. This is the ultimate goal of cooperation. If one person loves it but another does not, there's usually an underlying issue worth paying attention to. It likely means we haven't gone far enough and the work hasn't reached its full potential.

If one collaborator likes Choice A and another prefers Choice B, then the solution is not to choose A or B. It's to keep working until a Choice C is developed that both artists feel is superior. Choice C may incorporate elements of A, of B, of both, or of neither.

The moment one collaborator gives in and settles on a less preferential option for the sake of moving forward, everyone loses. Great decisions aren't made in a spirit of sacrifice. They're made by the mutual recognition of the best solution available.

If you already like the work in its current form, there's nothing to be lost by trying to better it until everyone loves it. You are not compromising. You are working together to surpass the current iteration.

$\odot$

We might not create equally with every partner. There can be incredibly talented people joining forces, yet for whatever reason, they don't resonate with each other. Or perhaps a participant doesn't work in the spirit of cooperation, and instead sets a tone of competition and persuasion.

If you never see eye to eye with a collaborator and after many iterations of the work can't arrive at something special, it might not be the right match.

At the same time, there may also be a misalignment if you *always* see eye to eye with a collaborator. We are not looking for someone who thinks like us, works like us, and shares our taste. If you and a collaborator agree on everything, then one of you may be unnecessary.

Imagine shining a beam of light through two filters of identical color. Whether apart or together, they produce the same hue. Whereas overlapping two contrasting filters produces a new shade.

In many of the greatest bands, collectives, and collaborations, a degree of polarity between members was part of the formula for greatness. The magic comes from a dynamic tension between different points of view, creating works more distinctive than a lone voice would.

Healthy tension in a collaboration is not uncommon. Friction allows the fire to come. As long as we're not attached to having it be our way, we welcome this friction. It's bringing us closer to the best version of the work at hand.

Some collaborations operate more like dictatorships than democracies. This system can work as well. In these cases, everyone agrees to line up behind one person's vision and do all they can to manifest it.

Whether the final decision is made by a single leader or a

collective, it's still a collaborative act. The participants are offering up their best work in the spirit of cooperation.

⊙

Communication is the core of skillful cooperation.

When giving feedback, don't make it personal. Always comment on the work itself and not the individual who made it. If a participant takes a critique personally, they tend to shut down.

Be as specific as possible with your feedback. Zoom in to discuss the details of what you're seeing and feeling. The more clinical the feedback, the better it will be received.

Saying, "I think the colors in these two areas don't interact well together," is more helpful than, "I don't like the colors."

Though you may have a specific fix in mind, hold back from sharing it immediately. The recipient may be able to come up with a better solution on their own.

When on the receiving end of feedback, our task is to set aside ego and work to fully understand the critique offered. When one participant suggests a specific detail that could be improved, we might mistakenly think that the entire work is being called into question. Our ego can perceive assistance as interference.

It helps to keep in mind that language is an imperfect means of communication. An idea is altered and diluted through its mistranslation into words. Those words are then further distorted through our filter as we take them in, leaving us in a world of ambiguity.

It requires patience and diligence to get past the story of what you think you're hearing and get close to understanding what's actually being said.

When receiving feedback, a useful practice is to repeat back the information. You may find that what you heard isn't what was said. And what was said may not even be what was actually meant.

Ask questions to gain clarity. When collaborators patiently explain what aspects of the work they're focusing on, we may recognize that our visions are not in opposition. We're just using different language or noticing different elements.

When sharing observations, specificity creates space. It dissipates the level of emotional charge and enables us to work together in service of the piece.

The synergy of a group
is as important—
if not more important—
than the talent
of the individuals.

The Sincerity Dilemma

Most artists overvalue sincerity.

They strive to create art that expresses their truth. The truest version of themselves.

Sincerity, however, is an elusive characteristic. It is different from other goals we may have. Where greatness is a target worthy of our aim, setting our sights on sincerity may be counterproductive. The more we stretch to reach it, the farther away it recedes. When a work presents itself as sincere, it can be seen as saccharine. Sweetness made small. A hollow rhyme in a greeting card.

In art, sincerity is a by-product. It cannot be the primary aim.

We like to think of ourselves as consistent, rational beings, possessing certain attributes and not others. Yet a person who is completely consistent, who possesses no contradictions, comes across as less real. Wooden. Plastic.

The most truthful and irrational aspects of ourselves are often hidden, and our access to them lies through the creation of art. Each work tells us who we are, often in ways the audience understands before we do.

Creativity is an exploratory process to find the concealed material within. We won't always discover it. If we do, it may not make sense. A seed could draw us because it contains something we don't understand, and this vague attraction will be as close to knowing as we ever get.

Some aspects of the self don't like to be approached head-on. They prefer to arrive indirectly, in their own way. As sudden glimpses caught in accidental moments, like sunlight glinting off the surface of a wave.

These apparitions don't fit into words that can easily be expressed in ordinary language. They're extra-ordinary. Beyond the mundane. A poem can convey information that can't be transmitted through prose or conversation.

And all art is poetry.

Art goes deeper than thought. Deeper than the stories

about yourself. It breaks through inner walls and accesses what's behind.

If we get out of the way and let the art do its work, it may yield the sincerity we seek. And sincerity may look nothing like we expected.

Anything that allows the audience
to access how you see the world
is accurate,
even if the information is wrong.

The Gatekeeper

No matter where your ideas come from or what they look like, they all eventually pass through a particular aspect of yourself: the editor, the gatekeeper.

This is who will determine the final expression of the work, regardless of how many selves were involved in its construction.

The editor's role is to gather and sift. Amplifying what's vital and whittling away the excess. Culling the work down to the best version of itself.

Sometimes the editor will find holes and send us out to gather data to fill them. Other times, there exists a wealth of information and the editor will remove what's unneeded to reveal the finished work.

Editing is a demonstration of taste. It isn't expressed through pointing to items we like: the music that pleases our ear or the films we revisit. Our taste is revealed in how our work is curated. What's included, what's not, and how the pieces are put together.

You may be drawn to different rhythms, colors, and patterns, though they might not live together harmoniously. The pieces must fit together in the container.

The container is the organizing principle of the work. It dictates which elements do and don't belong. The same furniture that suits a palace may not make sense in a monastery.

The editor is required to set ego aside. Ego pridefully attaches to individual elements of a work. The editor's role is to remain unattached and see beyond these passions to find unity and balance. Talented artists who are unskilled editors can do subpar work and fail to live up to their gift's promise.

Avoid confusing the editor's cold detachment with the inner critic. The critic doubts the work, undermines it, zooms in and picks it apart. The editor steps back, views the work holistically, and supports its full potential.

The editor is the professional in the poet.

As we move closer to the completion of a project, it can be helpful to drastically cut the work back to only what's necessary, to conduct *a ruthless edit.*

Much of the creative process thus far has been additive. So think of this as the subtractive part of the project. It typically occurs after all the building has been completed and the options exhausted.

Often, editing is thought of as trimming, cutting away the fat. In the ruthless edit, this is not the case. We are deciding what absolutely has to be there in order for the work to still be itself, what is completely necessary.

We are not aiming to reduce the work to its final length. We are working to reduce it beyond its final length. Even if trimming away 5 percent will leave the work at the scale you intend for it, we may cut deeper and leave only half or a third.

If you're working on a ten-song album and you've recorded twenty songs, you're not aiming to reduce it to ten. You're shrinking it to five, to only the tracks you can't live without.

If you've written a book that's over three hundred pages, try to reduce it to less than a hundred without losing its essence.

In addition to getting to the heart of the work, through this brutal edit we change our relationship to it. We come to understand its underlying structure and realize what truly matters, to disconnect from the attachment of making it and see it for what it is.

What effect does each component have? Does it amplify the essence? Does it distract from the essence? Does it contribute to the balance? Does it contribute to the structure? Is it absolutely necessary?

With the extra layers removed, you may stand back and notice that the work is successful as it is, in its simplest form. Or you may feel that you want to restore certain elements. As long as you're maintaining the integrity of the work, it's a matter of personal preference.

It's worth taking a moment to notice if any of your add-backs actually enhance the work. We're not looking for more for the sake of more. We're only looking for more for the sake of better.

The goal is to get the work to the point that when you see it, you know it couldn't have been arranged any other way. There's a sense of balance.

Of elegance.

It is not easy leaving behind elements you've put so much time and care into. Some artists fall in love with all the crafted material to the point where they resist letting go of an element even if the whole is better without it.

"Making the simple complicated is commonplace," Charles Mingus once said. "Making the complicated simple, awesomely simple, that's creativity."

Being an artist
means to be continually asking,
"How can it be better?"
whatever *it* is.
It may be your art,
and it may be your life.

Why Make Art?

(•)

As you deepen your participation in the creative act, you may come across a paradox.

Ultimately, the act of self-expression isn't really about you.

Most who choose the artist's path don't have a choice. We feel compelled to engage, as if by some primal instinct, the same force that calls turtles toward the sea after hatching in the sand.

We follow this instinct. To deny it is dispiriting, as if we are in violation of nature. If we zoom out, we see this blind impulse is always there, guiding our aim beyond ourselves.

In the moment when we feel the work is taking shape, there's a dynamic surge, followed by an urge to share, in the hopes of replicating that mysterious emotional charge in others.

This is the call to self-express, our creative purpose. It's not necessarily to understand ourselves or be understood. We share our filter, our way of seeing, in order to spark an echo in others. Art is a reverberation of an impermanent life.

As human beings, we come and go quickly, and we get to make works that stand as monuments to our time here. Enduring affirmations of existence. Michelangelo's *David*, the first cave paintings, a child's finger-paint landscapes—they all echo the same human cry, like graffiti scrawled in a bathroom stall:

I was here.

When you contribute your point of view to the world, others can see it. It's refracted through their filter and distributed again. This process is continuous and ongoing. Taken all together, it creates what we experience as reality.

Every work, no matter how trivial it may seem, plays a role in this greater cycle. The world continually unfolds. Nature renews itself. Art evolves.

Each of us has our own way of seeing this world. And this can lead to feelings of isolation. Art has an ability to connect us beyond the limitations of language.

Through this, we get to face our inner world outward, remove the boundaries of separation, and participate in the great remembering of what we came into this life knowing: There is no separation. We are one.

The reason we're alive
is to express ourselves in the world.
And creating art may be the most
effective and beautiful method of doing so.

Art goes beyond language, beyond lives.
It's a universal way to send messages
between each other and through time.

Harmony

(·)

The invisible threads of mathematics are laced through all natural beauty.

We can find the same ratios at work in the spirals of seashells and galaxies. In flower petals, DNA molecules, hurricanes, and the design of the human face.

Certain proportions create a sense of holy balance.

Our point of reference for beauty is nature. When we come upon these ratios when making art, they soothe us. Our creations are inspired by the relationships that we are most awed by.

The Parthenon, the Great Pyramid, Leonardo's *Vitruvian Man*, Brancusi's *Bird in Space*, Bach's *Goldberg Variations*, Beethoven's *Fifth Symphony*: these works all rely on the same geometry found in nature.

The universe holds a sense of harmony, a beautifully deep interdependent system. When you step back from a project you have been working on for some time and recognize a new symmetry you never knew was possible, you will likely feel a calm satisfaction. An excitement that contains at its core a sense of peace. Order appears. A harmonic resonance is palpable. You are a participant in this intricate mechanism.

In music, the rules of harmony are laid out in formulas. Each note has a vibrational wavelength, and every wavelength has a specific relationship to the others. Following mathematical principles, one can calculate harmonic pairings of these waves.

All elements have wavelengths: objects, colors, ideas. When we combine them, a new vibration is generated. Sometimes that vibration is harmonious, and other times it's dissonant.

We don't need to understand the math to create powerful work from these vibrations. For some, understanding the mathematics undermines their natural intuitive sense. We tune in to ourselves to feel harmony. We use the intellect in an attempt to explain it only after the fact.

For those who don't come to this knowing naturally, it

can be developed, given time. Through practiced atunement, you can grow alert to these natural resonances. More acutely sensing what's in balance and recognizing the divine proportions. When you're creating or completing a work, there's a clearer recognition, a harmonic ring. There's a sense of accord. A coherence. The individual elements merge and become one.

A great work doesn't have to be in harmony. Sometimes the point of the art is to show imbalance or to create a sense of unease.

In a song, when you hear a dissonant harmony suddenly fall in tune, there's a pleasing effect. That's why the discordant choice may be of interest. It creates tension and release, drawing our attention to the harmony we may not have otherwise noticed.

As we move deeper into alignment with fundamental harmonic principles in our craft, we might be able to recognize them everywhere we look. By working in the specific, our tastes become more refined in the general as well.

When we are unable to recognize the harmony in the universe around us, it's probably because we're not taking in enough data. If we zoom out or zoom in far enough, the integrated nature of all there is becomes clear.

Just as each small stroke on a canvas can't step aside to see the whole painting, we're unable to take in the great whole of relationships and counterbalance that surrounds us in all directions.

Our inability to comprehend the inner workings of the universe may actually bring us more in tune with its infinitude. The magic is not in the analyzing or the understanding. The magic lives in the wonder of what we do not know.

However you frame yourself as an artist,
the frame is too small.

What We Tell Ourselves

●

We have stories about ourselves,
and those are not who we are.
We have stories about the work,
and those are not what the work is.

All our efforts to make sense of ourselves and our art are
a smoke screen, an obfuscation. They don't illuminate what
is. They mislead us. We have no way of knowing what is insignificant and what is essential, or what our contributions
mean.

We tell ourselves varying stories of who we are and how
the work gets made. But none of them matter.

All that matters is the work itself. The art that actually gets made and how it's perceived.

You are you.

The work is the work.

Each person in the audience is themselves. Uniquely so.

None of it can truly be understood, let alone distilled to simple equations or common language.

Billions of data points are available at any given moment and we collect only a small number. With this glimpse through a keyhole, we assemble an interpretation and add another story to our collection.

With each story we tell ourselves, we negate possibility. Reality is diminished. Rooms of the self are walled off. Truth collapses to fit a fictional organizing principle we've adopted.

As artists, we're called to let go of these stories, again and again, and blindly put our faith in the curious energy drawing us down the path.

The artwork is the point where all the elements come together—the universe, the prism of self, the magic and discipline of transmuting idea to flesh. And if these lead you into contradiction—into territories that seem unbridgeable or unknowable—that doesn't mean they aren't harmonious.

Even in perceived chaos, there is order and pattern. A cosmic undercurrent running through all things, which no story is immense enough to contain.